Can De-Industrialisation Seriously Damage Your Wealth?

*A Review of Why Growth Rates Differ
and How to Improve Economic Performance*

N. F. R. CRAFTS

*Professor of Economic History,
University of Warwick*

IEA

Published by

INSTITUTE OF ECONOMIC AFFAIRS
1993

First published in January 1993

by

THE INSTITUTE OF ECONOMIC AFFAIRS

2 Lord North Street, Westminster,
London SW1P 3LB

© THE INSTITUTE OF ECONOMIC AFFAIRS 1993

Hobart Paper 120

ISSN 0073-2818
ISBN 0-255 36316-8

The Institute gratefully acknowledges financial support for its publications programme and other work from a generous benefaction by the late Alec and Beryl Warren.

Printed in Great Britain by
GORON PRO-PRINT CO LTD
6 Marlborough Road, Churchill Industrial Estate, Lancing, W. Sussex
Text set in Berthold Baskerville

CONTENTS

		page
FOREWORD	*Colin Robinson*	7
THE AUTHOR		9

I. INTRODUCTION 11
Economic Growth in the OECD Since 1870 12
The Sources of Growth 13
Maddison's Growth Accounting Methodology 14
Relative Economic Decline in the UK 18
De-Industrialisation 20

II. WHY GROWTH RATES DIFFER: A REVIEW OF
SOME HYPOTHESES 25
Macro-Structuralist Models 25
(i) The Thirlwall Hypothesis 25
(ii) Bacon and Eltis: 'Too Few Producers' 26
(iii) Kaldor's Formulation 27
'Catch-Up' and Convergence 29
The Role of Convergence in Growth 31
New Growth Economics 33
The Romer Approach 34
The Lucas Model 35
Policy Implications 38

III. BRITISH ECONOMIC GROWTH BEFORE AND
AFTER 1979 39
Was Growth Performance Better in the 1980s? 39
'Measurable Economic Welfare' 41
Slow Growth in the 'Golden Age', 1950-73 44
Role of 'Long-termist' Investments in Germany 44
'Behavioural Differences' 45

'Competition Policy'   46
Weakness in British Nationalised Industries   47
A Renaissance in the 1980s?   49
British Technology Weakness Continues   50
No Return to the 1970s   51

IV. DOES DE-INDUSTRIALISATION JEOPARDISE FUTURE
    GROWTH PROSPECTS?   53
Recent Developments in Britain's External
    Trade and Payments Position   53
Macro-economic Policy's Effects on
    the Balance of Payments   54
A Balance-of-Payments Constraint on Growth?   59
Learning Effects, Externalities and Future
    Technological Capabilities   60
Empirical Support for Krugman-Lucas—
    'Special Cases'   61
Conclusions   63

V. DO WE NEED A NEW INDUSTRIAL POLICY?   64
Market Distortions, Macro-Policy and
    the 'House of Lords View'   64
Government Policy 'Idiosyncratic'   65
Market Failure as a Justification for
    Industrial Policy   65
Past Experience of Industrial Policy   68
Failure of Industrial Policy:
    European Examples   69
Current Industrial Policies   70
EC Moves to Encourage Collaboration in
    High-Tech Industries   72
Conclusions   73
Short-Termism   74

VI. CONCLUSIONS   76

GLOSSARY   78

QUESTIONS FOR DISCUSSION   81

REFERENCES/FURTHER READING   82

SUMMARY   *Back cover*

LIST OF TABLES:

Table 1:   Growth Rates of Real GDP per Head of
           Population, 1870-1989   12

Table 2:   Labour Productivity Growth, 1950-87   13

Table 3:   The Sources of Economic Growth, 1950-73
           and 1973-87   15

Table 4:   Employment Structure and Sectoral
           Contributions to Productivity Growth,
           1913-50, 1950-73 and 1973-87   16

Table 5:   GDP per Person Employed (UK=100),
           1870-1987   18

Table 6:   Manufacturing Output per Person Employed
           (UK=100), 1869-1989   19

Table 7:   Shares of World Trade in Manufactures,
           1937-1990   20

Table 8:   Changes in Real Incomes and
           Industrialisation Levels, 1973 and 1989   21

Table 9:   Growth Rates of Manufacturing Output,
           1950-73, 1973-89 and 1979-89   22

Table 10: Balance of Trade as % of GDP, 1952-89   23

Table 11: Growth Rate of Real GDP/Hour Worked:
           Actual and Potential Bonus from Catch-Up
           and Reconstruction, 1950-60, 1960-73 and
           1979-88   30

Table 12: Actual and Forecast Convergence,
           1950-1986/7   32

Table 13: Productivity in the Business Sector, 1960-1989   40

Table 14: Regression Estimates of 'Residual Growth',
           1950-60, 1960-73 and 1979-88   41

Table 15: Growth of Measurable Economic Welfare/
           Head, 1950-73 and 1979-89   42

Table 16: Labour Productivity Comparisons in
           International Companies: Reasons for
           Productivity Differentials, 1972   46

[5]

Table 17: Productivity Outcomes in UK Nationalised/
Privatised Sector, 1968-78 and 1979-88   48

Table 18: Revealed Comparative Advantage in
High-Technology Industries:
Selected Countries, 1979 and 1988   56

Table 19: Terms-of-Trade Adjustments to Real GDP
Growth, 1950-73 and 1973-87   58

Table 20: Value Added in High-Technology Industry,
1979 and 1988   62

Table 21: DTI Expenditure (£ million, 1988-9 prices),
1981/2, 1986/7 and 1990/1   71

LIST OF FIGURES:

Figure 1: Short- and Long-Run Specialisation in
International Trade
    (a) Short-Run   36
    (b) Long-Run   37

Figure 2: Subsidised Entry into the Civil
Airliner Market
    (i) Successful Intervention   66
    (ii) Unsuccessful Intervention   67

LIST OF BOXES:

Box 1: The Krugman-Lucas Model   36-37
Box 2: Rent-Snatching through Subsidies   66-67

FOREWORD

For years economists and industrialists have agonised over the relatively slow growth of the British economy and about the consequences for growth of 'de-industrialisation'. During the Thatcher boom years, anxiety about Britain's relative economic decline receded but, not surprisingly, it re-emerged as the economy moved into recession.

Some of the explanations offered for Britain's poor performance probably command wide support among industrialists—for instance, that British governments (central and local) have inadvertently hampered industry by excessive regulation (for health and safety, environmental, local planning and other reasons), by trying to fix exchange rates and by generally poor macro-economic management. Another school of thought—which seems to be gaining ground both in Britain and in the United States—claims that government should positively promote manufacturing and other industrial activities, if necessary by trade protection. Reports by House of Lords Committees have, in recent years, put forward such views.

In Hobart Paper No. 120, Professor Nick Crafts, a distinguished economic historian from the University of Warwick, examines the evidence about growth rates (economy-wide and in industry) in Britain as compared with other countries and also considers the case for an 'industrial policy' which promotes British manufacturing industry.

He begins with a careful analysis of how (Section I) and why (Section II) growth rates differ. Professor Crafts demonstrates the long-term nature of relative economic decline in Britain, which has taken place over a century or more, but he shows also that there was some revival in the 1980s (especially of manufacturing output). The main 'industrial' problem which emerged in the 1980s was a significant deterioration in the manufacturing trade balance. Some economists have claimed that government should help manufacturers by subsidies for investment, protection for 'infant industries' and intervention to correct 'market failures'. Yet, as Professor Crafts says, such policies have the

'... hallmarks of British industrial policy during the "picking

[7]

winners" years of the 1960s and 1970s when relative economic decline was at its most virulent'. (p. 38)

In Section III, Professor Crafts shows that the relatively slow growth of the British economy up to 1979 was a consequence of an environment which

'. . . encouraged the survival of the inefficient and created a situation where the bargaining power of those seeking to block productivity-enhancing change was often considerable'. (p. 49)

Under the Thatcher administrations of the 1980s, however, some of the obstacles to growth were diminished and

'. . . the UK performed a somewhat belated catching-up exercise associated with the switch in policy régime'. (p. 50)

Professor Crafts turns, in Sections IV, V and VI, to an analysis of whether de-industrialisation has adverse long-run implications and of whether return to a 'high-profile industrial policy' (p. 63) would help. He argues that there is considerable scope for eliminating policy errors by government but that interventionist industrial policies may well impose costs which exceed any benefits they bring. Present problems stem

'. . . largely from macro-economic mistakes in exchange rate/interest rate policies which first require to be corrected rather than being compounded by distortions introduced into micro-economic policy'. (p. 76)

Productivity growth was significantly increased in the Thatcher years and it is therefore 'important not to return to the *status quo ante* 1979' (p. 77). Intervention is only too likely to reduce the pressure on firms to reduce costs. Professor Crafts sees scope for government action to 'reduce short-termism and to strengthen human capital formation' but he warns that such action should ensure that the 'disciplines of competition' are retained (p. 77).

The views expressed in this Hobart Paper are those of the author, not of the Institute (which has no corporate view), its Trustees, Directors or Advisers. The paper is published as a careful and stimulating analysis of Britain's economic performance and of policy proposals designed to improve that performance.

January 1993   COLIN ROBINSON
Editorial Director, Institute of Economic Affairs;
University of Surrey

[8]

THE AUTHOR

NICK (N. F. R.) CRAFTS has been Professor of Economic History at the University of Warwick since 1988. Previously he was Fellow and Praelector in Economics at University College, Oxford (1977-86), Visiting Professor of Economics at Stanford University (1982-3) and Professor of Economic History at the University of Leeds (1987-8).

He was born in 1949 and educated at Brunts Grammar School, Mansfield, and Trinity College, Cambridge. Professor Crafts's publications include *British Economic Growth During the Industrial Revolution* (1985) and articles in many journals including *Economic History Review*, *Economic Journal*, *Economic Policy*, *Economica*, *Journal of Economic History*, *Oxford Economic Papers*, *Population Studies*, etc. He has recently edited and contributed to *The British Economy Since 1945* (1991) (with N. Woodward) and *Britain in the International Economy 1870-1939* (1992) (with S. Broadberry). He is a member of the Council of the Economic History Society and of the Council of the Royal Economic Society and is a Fellow of the British Academy (elected 1992).

I. INTRODUCTION

It is widely believed that manufacturing is of crucial and special importance to the achievement of rapid and sustained economic growth in the UK. The hypothesis usually carries with it the proposition that future growth prospects are much weakened by the recent reductions in the extent of manufacturing, particularly in the 1980s. Several recent reports from House of Lords Select Committees have asserted similar claims. Here is an example:

> 'Manufacturing industry is vital to the prosperity of the United Kingdom ... Our manufacturing base is dangerously small; to achieve adequate growth from such a small base will be difficult' (House of Lords, 1991, p. 3).

Many politicians, including the President of the Board of Trade (Heseltine, 1987), share these beliefs and presume that they create a case for an 'industrial policy'. Some economists promote protectionist policies to redress the situation (Thirlwall and Gibson, 1992, pp. 381-83).

This study reviews the part played by manufacturing in British economic growth in order to assess the experience of the 1980s and to consider policies which might improve medium-term growth prospects. It seems opportune to take a new look at these issues not only because of the insights which can be obtained from the 'Thatcher Experiment' but also because the 'new growth economics' literature, which has burgeoned since the mid-1980s, offers some new theoretical insights which ostensibly might be used to support proposals for a return to inter-ventionism to pursue growth through a policy of promoting manufacturing.

This section seeks to establish the empirical background for the analysis which follows by placing the UK's long-term growth record in an international context and examining comparative experience in de-industrialisation. The data are, of course, estimates rather than facts but they can bear the weight of interpretation placed on them.[1]

---

[1] In what follows the debt that all economic historians owe to the Herculean labours of Angus Maddison will be apparent.

TABLE 1

GROWTH RATES OF REAL GDP PER HEAD
OF POPULATION, 1870-1989

(annual average compound growth rates)
(per cent)

	1870-1913	1913-50	1950-73	1973-89
Australia	0·9	0·7	2·4	1·7
Austria	1·5	0·2	4·9	2·4
Belgium	1·0	0·7	3·5	2·0
Canada	2·3	1·5	2·9	2·5
Denmark	1·6	1·5	3·1	1·6
Finland	1·4	1·9	4·3	2·7
France	1·3	1·1	4·0	1·8
Germany	1·6	0·7	4·9	2·1
Italy	1·3	0·8	5·0	2·6
Japan	1·4	0·9	8·0	3·1
Netherlands	1·0	1·1	3·4	1·4
Norway	1·3	2·1	3·2	3·6
Sweden	1·5	2·1	3·3	1·8
Switzerland	1·2	2·1	3·1	1·0
UK	**1·0**	**0·8**	**2·5**	**1·8**
USA	1·8	1·6	2·2	1·6

Source: Maddison (1991, p. 49).

Economic Growth in the OECD Since 1870

The growth record of the group of 16 advanced countries whose experience has been closely analysed by Maddison (1991) is summarised in Table 1.

The overall pattern is fairly well-known; key points to note are as follows:

○ The years after the Second World War stand out as an epoch of exceptionally rapid growth; the UK, in common with other OECD countries, saw the fastest increase in living standards in its economic history.

○ Growth since 1973 has slowed down substantially in virtually

TABLE 2

LABOUR PRODUCTIVITY GROWTH, 1950-87

(annual average compound growth rates)
(per cent)

	Whole Economy	*Industry*
1950-73		
France	4·61	5·2
Germany	4·84	5·6
Japan	7·57	9·5
UK	**2·54**	**2·9**
USA	2·14	2·2
1973-87		
France	2·14	3·9
Germany	1·80	2·0
Japan	2·89	3·9
UK	**1·75**	**2·8**
USA	0·58	1·1

Source: Maddison (1991, pp. 134, 150, 158-59).

all countries in the Table; nevertheless it compares favourably in most cases with pre-1950 experience.

○ The range of growth rates has tended to be larger since 1950; moreover, positions in the 'league table' have changed over time.

○ The relatively poor showing of the UK is clear throughout. How far this relative economic decline was reversed during the 1980s, which are not shown separately in Maddison's work, is discussed in Sections III and IV.

The Sources of Growth

Growth of real GDP per person is, of course, very closely related to the growth of output per person employed—differing only to the extent that the proportion of the population employed changes over time. Table 2 confirms that the difference is usually, though not always, small. The Table also demonstrates that the post-war national accounts data generally show a faster growth of labour productivity in industry than in the rest of the economy.

Labour productivity growth is influenced by many variables but the main proximate influences are capital accumulation, technological progress, acquisition of skills, scale economies and improvements in the utilisation of resources. A further step in describing the sources of growth can be taken through 'growth accounting', a technique which attempts to measure the contributions of various sources of growth and which has come to be used widely in the past quarter-century. It formed the basis of a seminal study of long-run British economic growth by Matthews *et al.* (1982).[1] An analysis of this kind recently carried out by Maddison is summarised in Table 3. *Total factor productivity (TFP)** growth is responsible for the increases in output over and above those resulting from additional quantities of capital and labour. In the original applications of this approach the extra output might have resulted from improvements in the quality of the factors, reductions in inefficiency or better techniques. Maddison's approach, however, seeks to include improvements in quality in measuring the growth of capital and labour; thus TFP growth is primarily seen as the result of elimination of inefficiencies in the use of resources and of technological change.

Maddison's Growth Accounting Methodology

A number of quite serious difficulties arise in Maddison's methodology which are discussed fully in Crafts (1992) and briefly in Section II. Nevertheless, despite these problems, the main messages of Table 3 seem robust. They are:

○ The achievement of very rapid growth rates by OECD

[1] The methodology decomposes the rate of growth into contributions from the inputs of capital and labour and from total factor productivity growth as in equation (1):

$$\Delta Y/Y = a\Delta K/K + \beta\Delta L/L + \Delta TFP/TFP \qquad (1)$$

where α and β are the elasticities of output of capital and labour respectively, conventionally approximated by the shares of profits and wages in national income. This approximation is justified by recognising that the contribution of growth in factor supply to growth in output depends on marginal product; thus for capital $\Delta Y = \Delta Y/\Delta K \cdot \Delta K$. Divide both sides by Y and multiply the right-hand side top and bottom by K to obtain $\Delta Y/Y = (\Delta Y/\Delta K \cdot K/Y) \Delta K/K$. If capital receives its marginal product the term in brackets is the share of profits.

*Words and phrases set in italics and followed by an asterisk are defined/explained in the 'Glossary', below, pp. 78-80.

TABLE 3

THE SOURCES OF ECONOMIC GROWTH,
1950-73 AND 1973-87

(annual average compound growth rates)
(per cent per annum)

	Capital	Labour	Total Factor Productivity	GDP Growth
1950-73				
France	1·84	0·18	3·02	5·04
Germany	2·27	0·15	3·50	5·92
Japan	2·93	1·63	4·71	9·27
UK	**1·75**	**0·01**	**1·27**	**3·03**
USA	1·37	1·17	1·11	3·65
1973-87				
France	1·48	–0·24	0·92	2·16
Germany	1·28	–0·49	1·01	1·80
Japan	2·29	0·66	0·78	3·73
UK	**1·12**	**–0·19**	**0·82**	**1·75**
USA	1·24	1·31	–0·04	2·51

Source: Adapted from Maddison (1991, p. 134, pp. 158-59).

countries has relied heavily on total factor productivity growth rather than simply on high rates of physical investment.

o The slowdown in growth since 1973 is, in every case but that of the UK, more than 50 per cent due to a slowdown in total factor productivity growth.

o The very weak growth performance in the UK compared with France and Germany in the period 1950-73 was largely attributable to differences in total factor productivity growth. (A similar analysis confined to manufacturing comparing the UK and Germany produced exactly the same finding (Panic, 1976).) Faster Japanese growth has entailed greater reliance on factor inputs, especially since 1973.

Such exercises in growth accounting are at best guides to the

TABLE 4

EMPLOYMENT STRUCTURE AND SECTORAL CONTRIBUTIONS TO PRODUCTIVITY GROWTH, 1913-50, 1950-73 AND 1973-87

(per cent)

	Agriculture	Industry	Services
1913-50			
France	19·3 (28)	66·5 (35)	14·2 (37)
Germany	−8·0 (22)	123·2 (43)	−15·2 (35)
Japan	8·3 (48)	77·2 (23)	14·5 (29)
UK	**12·9 (5)**	**56·7 (47)**	**30·4 (48)**
USA	9·0 (13)	47·1 (33)	43·9 (54)
1950-73			
France	9·8 (11)	49·1 (40)	41·1 (49)
Germany	4·3 (7)	62·4 (48)	33·3 (45)
Japan	6·4 (13)	65·2 (37)	28·4 (49)
UK	**5·1 (3)**	**46·2 (43)**	**48·7 (54)**
USA	11·6 (4)	41·0 (33)	47·4 (63)
1973-87			
France	7·9 (7)	52·7 (30)	39·4 (63)
Germany	3·6 (5)	52·7 (40)	43·7 (55)
Japan	3·6 (8)	61·4 (34)	35·0 (58)
UK	**4·0 (2)**	**50·9 (30)**	**45·1 (68)**
USA	9·2 (3)	45·0 (27)	45·8 (70)

Note and Sources: Contributions are calculated according to the standard formula in Nordhaus (1972) using terminal weights and are expressed as percentages of intrasectoral productivity change. Data are taken from Maddison (1991, pp. 150-51, 248-49) and OECD (1991a). Figures in parentheses are percentages of employment in the terminal year. 'Industry' includes gas, electricity, water and construction as well as manufacturing.

rôle of supply-side factors in growth and ignore demand. This is appropriate as a first approximation when studying medium-and long-term trends, since we would expect *Keynesian demand shocks** primarily to influence short-run cycles. Some refinements of this position are, however, explored in Section II. More importantly, in Section II the determinants of these proximate sources of growth are explored.

It is frequently argued that a concentration on manufacturing is more conducive to faster labour productivity growth than would be obtained by an economy devoted to service sector activity. This is often singled out as a reason why 'manufacturing matters' (Mayes, 1987, p. 47). To examine this suggestion initially, Table 4 sets out an alternative accounting decomposition of the sources of productivity growth using a standard formula.

Table 4 confirms that industry has contributed a large, though not overwhelming, share of 20th-century productivity change in the most advanced countries. Moreover, the data suggest that industry's share of productivity growth has tended generally to be distinctly larger than its share of employment such that, *prima facie*, a de-industrialisation of employment would seem likely to slow down future productivity growth.

The validity of this inference is further discussed in Section IV. At this stage, however, it is important to bear in mind that the apparent difference between service sector and industrial productivity growth is to an extent an illusion resulting from measurement difficulties. In particular, some aspects of service sector output growth (mostly in the relatively expanding category of 'public and professional services') are conventionally estimated as equal to employment growth—that is to say, productivity growth is *assumed* to be zero. Increasing evidence indicates that these sectors do experience labour productivity growth so that the conventional assumption is too pessimistic (Levitt and Joyce, 1987, ch. 6). Millward (1990) has plausibly suggested, on the basis of such measurement as has been possible, that it might be better to approximate the output of public and professional services on the assumption that capital rather than labour productivity is constant over time. If this proposal is correct, the contributions of industry and services to productivity growth in the UK were 39·7 and 55·8 per cent respectively in 1950-73 (rather than the 46·2 and 48·7 recorded in Table 4) and 51·2 and 45·3 per cent respectively in 1973-87 (rather than 50·9 and 45·1). Thus, in 1950-73 the contribution of industry appears to have been significantly *less* than in Table 4, whereas in 1973-87 the changed assumption makes little difference.

[17]

TABLE 5

GDP PER PERSON EMPLOYED (UK = 100), 1870-1987

	USA/UK	Germany/UK	France/UK
1870	95·1	48·8	53·0
1890	98·1	53·3	52·5
1913	127·9	64·1	61·7
1929	154·0	64·3	72·7
1938	143·0	74·9	70·0
1950	167·4	63·3	69·7
1960	167·5	90·2	88·6
1973	151·6	104·7	110·2
1987	128·9	105·6	116·4

Source: Maddison (1991, pp. 198, 268).

Note: Comparisons for each year with the UK; changes in position between years reflect relative growth not absolute levels of performance.

Relative Economic Decline in the UK

The relatively slow growth and, especially, slow productivity growth in the UK reported in Tables 1-3 has led over the long term to levels of productivity and living standards falling below those abroad. Tables 5 and 6 reflect this relative economic decline. Both tables make comparisons which attempt to adjust prevailing exchange rates for differences in purchasing power. The possibilities of measurement error are considerable. Allowing for quality differences in ostensibly similar products is always open to doubt. Nevertheless, the message from these tables is in broad outline probably reliable.

The key points from Tables 5 and 6 taken together are:

○ For the whole economy (Table 5), the UK's productivity exceeded those of France and Germany until sometime in the 1960s but now lags somewhat. The USA was far ahead of all Europeans in the 1950s since when its productivity lead, even against Britain, has fallen sharply.

○ Until very recently, there was a clear tendency for the productivity gap between the UK and the other countries to be distinctly larger in manufacturing than in the economy as a whole (Table 6).

[18]

TABLE 6

MANUFACTURING OUTPUT PER PERSON EMPLOYED
(UK = 100), 1869-1989[a]

	USA/UK	Germany/UK	France/UK
1869	203·8		
1875		100·0	
1879	187·8		
1882		83·6	
1885		94·5	
1889	195·4	94·7	
1896	181·4	103·3	64·3
1899	194·8	99·0	
1907	192·0 (201·9)	106·4	(64·0)
1913	212·9	119·0	79·3
1920	222·8		
1924	221·0		77·5
1925	234·2	95·2	
1929	249·9	104·7	82·3
1935	207·8	*102·0 (102·0)	
1937	*208·3 (208·3)	99·9	
1938	191·6	107·1	76·3
1949	249·0		83·0
1950	262·6 (273·4)	96·0 (99·5)	83·9
1958	250·0	111·1	91·1
1968	242·6 (272·7)	120·0 (130·4)	109·1
1975	207·5 (224·7)	132·9	124·0
1977	229·6 (251·0)	148·6	138·2
1980	192·8	140·2	138·8
1984	183·3	122·7	*120·4 (120·4)
1987	188·8 (186·6)	107·8 (112·7)	112·1
1988	184·0	105·9	112·2
1989	177·0	105·1	

[a] Years for which data available.

Source and Notes: Based on Broadberry (1992a); comparisons are extrapolated using domestic growth data from benchmark comparisons in years marked *. Other available benchmark comparisons recorded in parentheses as cross-check on accuracy.

[19]

TABLE 7

SHARES OF WORLD TRADE IN MANUFACTURES,
1937-1990

(per cent)

	1937	1950	1960	1970	1979	1990
France	5·8	9·9	9·6	8·7	10·5	9·7
Germany	21·8	7·3	19·3	19·8	20·9	20·2
Japan	6·9	3·4	6·9	11·7	13·7	15·9
UK	**20·9**	**25·5**	**16·5**	**10·8**	**9·1**	**8·6**
USA	19·2	27·3	21·6	18·6	16·0	16·0

Sources: Brown and Sheriff (1979), CSO (1991), Maizels (1963).

○ Exceptionally poor productivity performance in British manufacturing relative to France and Germany is a striking feature of the period from the 1950s through the 1970s. The British manufacturing productivity revival of the 1980s also stands out in Table 6.

○ The superiority of American labour productivity in manufacturing (Table 6) is seen to be of very long standing.

Relative economic decline has been a persistent feature of British experience over the last century. Nevertheless, it was clearly at its most acute in the three decades after 1950.

De-Industrialisation
The long-run process of economic development entails substantial structural changes in all economies. Differences in sectoral productivity growth rates and income elasticities of demand, together with shifts of comparative advantage, all play a part. Indeed, recognising the importance of specialisation in international trade implies that there is no presumption that all countries should be equally 'industrial' in an efficient world allocation of resources.

World trade patterns have changed considerably over time (Table 7). The share of world manufactured exports originating in the UK has been in decline for many years, especially during the fast-growth 1950s and 1960s, suggesting a loss of competitiveness. The most obvious, and most frequently drawn,

TABLE 8

CHANGES IN REAL INCOMES AND INDUSTRIALISATION LEVELS, 1973 AND 1989

	1973			1989		
	Income/ Head	% Employed in Industry	% Value Added from Industry	Income/ Head	% Employed in Industry	% Value Added from Industry
Australia	10,331	35·4	38·1	13,584	26·5	31·0
Austria	8,644	43·0	42·6	12,585	37·0	36·1
Belgium	9,416	41·5	40·4	12,876	28·5	30·2
Canada	11,866	30·6	32·4	17,576	25·7	30·0
Denmark	10,527	33·8	28·1	13,514	27·4	24·0
Finland	9,072	35·7	36·3	13,934	31·0	31·4
France	10,323	39·7	38·1	13,837	30·1	28·9
Germany	10,110	47·5	47·0	13,989	39·8	39·3
Italy	8,568	39·2	42·2	12,955	32·4	33·8
Japan	9,237	37·2	46·3	15,101	34·3	41·6
Netherlands	10,267	36·5	38·0	12,737	26·5	30·8
Norway	9,346	33·9	33·2	16,500	25·3	35·4
Sweden	11,292	36·8	34·8	14,912	29·4	30·8
UK	10,063	42·6	38·4	13,468	29·4	29·5
USA	14,103	33·2	34·1	18,317	26·7	29·2

Sources: Income levels are measured in US dollars at 1985 prices adjusted for differences in the purchasing power of currencies, and are from Maddison (1991, pp. 6-7); industrialisation levels are from OECD (1991a).

contrast is with Germany which now has a similar proportion of world trade to what it had in 1937 (and even 1913). At the same time, Germany's trade share is itself unusual, as is suggested by the similarity in recent years of the British and French percentages of exports.

Table 8 is concerned with de-industrialisation as it is most commonly defined—a decline in the proportion of employment in industry as a whole. It shows:

○ Throughout the OECD growth since 1973 has entailed a significant de-industrialisation of employment. The UK has, however, experienced considerably higher than average de-industrialisation. Belgium is the only other country in the Table which has de-industrialised to a comparable extent.

○ Nevertheless, in the late 1980s the UK had much the same proportion of the labour force in industry as several other European countries with a similar level of income per head—for example, Belgium, France and the Netherlands.

○ Germany and Japan are the most 'industrial' of the countries in Table 8, as would be expected given their shares of world trade (Table 7).[1] The relatively high industrialisation of German employment in 1989 is clearly seen to be atypical.

The revival of manufacturing productivity performance in the

TABLE 9

GROWTH RATES OF MANUFACTURING OUTPUT

(per cent per annum)

	1950-73	1973-89	1979-89
France	6·7	1·6	0·6
Germany	7·8	1·1	0·8
Japan	15·0	4·7	5·6
UK	**3·1**	**0·5**	**1·2**
USA	4·6	2·9	3·0

Sources: OECD (1991a), OECD (1970), Minami (1986, p. 103), United States (1992).

[1] The USA, while having a similar share of world trade to Japan, is of course a much larger economy.

UK in the 1980s was much more impressive than the growth of output. There was, of course, a drastic shedding of labour as Britain moved closer to best-practice European manning levels. Since 1973 growth of UK manufacturing output has not kept pace with that of France or Germany, although, as Table 9 shows, the difference is fairly small compared with 1950-73. Moreover, in the 10 years to 1989 UK manufacturing output growth was faster than in those countries. The manufacturing base seems not to have contracted so much relatively to that of other European countries as is sometimes thought.

All in all, then, on the indicators examined above, UK de-industrialisation does not appear to be far out of line with the wider European experience. Table 10, however, shows the uncommon feature of recent developments relating to British manufacturing, and reveals the factor which has so worried House of Lords Select Committees, namely the trend in the balance of manufacturing trade. Up to the end of the 1970s, as Rowthorn and Wells (1987) emphasise, the UK was characterised by roughly offsetting but unusually large movements in

TABLE 10

BALANCE OF TRADE AS PERCENTAGE OF GDP

	1952	1973	1979	1989
(a) *Manufactures*				
France	+3·9	+1·5	+2·5	−0·9
Germany	+7·5	+8·8	+8·2	+9·2
Japan	+5·2	+6·0	+7·5	+5·9
UK	**+9·1**	**+2·0**	**+1·4**	**−3·6**
USA	+1·8	+0·0	+0·0	−2·3
(b) *Non-Manufactured Goods and Services*				
France	−4·9	−1·6	−2·8	−0·2
Germany	−6·8	−7·5	−8·0	−2·6
Japan	−8·4	−6·3	−8·4	−3·2
UK	**−10·8**	**−4·5**	**−1·3**	**−1·3**
USA	−0·6	+0·0	−1·7	+0·0

Sources: Rowthorn and Wells (1987, pp. 64-67); OECD (1991a).

manufacturing and non-manufacturing trade associated with a substantial change in the UK's specialisation in tradeable goods production. In the business cycle of the 1980s, however, the deterioration in manufacturing trade was not offset in this way.

The change in the UK's manufacturing trade position since 1952 is indeed remarkable. Its implications are discussed in Sections II, III and IV, but two preliminary observations can usefully be made here.

(i) Tables 7 and 10 together show that the major recent change is in import penetration of manufactures into the UK rather than loss of UK world market share in manufactured exports. Whereas imports were less than 5 per cent of home demand for manufactures in the early 1950s, they had risen to 16 per cent by the early 1970s and to over 35 per cent by the late 1980s (Crafts and Woodward, 1991, p. 16).

(ii) There has been a notable change in the UK's international trading position. To some it is obvious that this will have adverse effects on future growth prospects: 'sustainable growth has not been possible and will not be possible without a favourable trade balance in manufactures' (House of Lords, 1985, p. 42). Yet before this proposition is accepted uncritically, it ought to be examined in an explicit context of growth theory and of the sources of economic growth. How does Table 10 relate to Tables 1, 2 and 3?

II. WHY GROWTH RATES DIFFER:
A REVIEW OF SOME HYPOTHESES

This section examines certain basic theoretical ideas which help to clarify the links between manufacturing and economic growth. Some initial evidence relating to the plausibility of different schools of thought is presented but more detailed analysis of British experience and prospects is left to Sections III and IV. Growth economics is once again the focus of much research effort after a long period of neglect by theorists.

Macro-Structuralist Models

In the 1960s and 1970s a number of British economists drew attention to structural aspects of the economy which were held to be comparatively unfavourable to growth. Three of these deserve attention: the balance-of-payments constraint associated with Thirlwall (1979), the 'too-few-producers' hypothesis popularised by Bacon and Eltis (1976), and the *Verdoorn's Law**approach propounded by Kaldor (1966). Each can be seen as a variant of theoretical elaborations of the House of Lords Select Committee's view that erosion of the manufacturing base jeopardises future growth.

(i) The Thirlwall Hypothesis

The balance-of-payments constraint revolves around the relative demand for exports and imports. Under this approach, a calculation is made of the maximum home growth consistent with maintaining balance on the current account of the balance of payments assuming no changes in the real exchange rate (international competitiveness). This maximum rate of growth will be lower the less income growth promotes export demand and the more it promotes expenditure on imports. The constraint will be binding if the maximum growth permitted is lower than the growth of productive potential.

It was frequently suggested in the 1970s that the demand conditions facing Britain were much less favourable than those elsewhere, presumably because of an unfavourable manufacturing product range. Thirlwall (1979) argued that the *income*

[25]

elasticity of demand* for British exports was less than Britain's income elasticity of demand for imports,[1] so that a tendency existed for imports to rise faster than exports. Moreover, this tendency could not be offset by devaluation because, according to Thirlwall, changing the real exchange rate was not feasible. This argument seems, however, both to have exaggerated the tightness of any short-term balance-of-payments constraint on growth and to have been erroneous as applied to the long term. With the passage of time two points, in particular, now seem much clearer.

(i)   Better econometric evidence is now available on the trade elasticities which show much smaller differences between countries and smaller absolute values for the differences between the export and import *income elasticities** $(e_x - e_m)$.[2]

(ii)   Orthodox neo-classical economics predicts that, if the real exchange rate is free to vary (that is, balance-of-payments difficulties can be resolved by a rising relative price of imports), then the consequences of unfavourable demand elasticities would be felt on the terms of trade but not on GDP growth. The hypothesised inflexibility of the real exchange rate was attributed to 'real wage rigidity' (that is, domestic wages always rise enough to negate the gains to competitiveness from exchange rate adjustments), in a heavily unionised environment. This is not borne out by the evidence; for example, OECD (1989, p. 35) presents data which show that neither the UK nor other OECD economies were characterised by long-run real wage rigidity in the 1970s and 1980s.

(ii) Bacon and Eltis: 'Too Few Producers'

Bacon and Eltis's (1976) 'too few producers' explanation of slowing UK growth distinguished between the 'marketed' and

[1] The basic source of the balance-of-payments constraint on growth can be portrayed by the following simple formula:

$$\Delta Y / Y_h = (\Delta Y / Y_{rw} \cdot e_x) / e_m \qquad (2)$$

where Y is output, h is home, rw is the rest of the world, e_x and e_m are respectively the income elasticities of the world's demand for home exports and of the home country's demand for imports. According to Thirlwall, $e_x - e_m$ was -0.65 for the UK compared with 0.19 for Germany and 2.32 for Japan.

[2] For the UK, OECD estimated a value of -0.11 in the mid-1970s and -0.10 in the mid-1980s, while for Germany the figures were 0.18 and 0.25 respectively and for Japan 0.30 and 0.29 (OECD, 1989, p. 129).

'non-marketed' sectors of the economy rather than between manufacturing and services—manufacturing is a subset of the marketed sector while the non-marketed sector essentially reflects the activities of the state. They argued that the surplus of output over consumption in the marketed sector was potentially available for net exports, or investment in the marketed sector, or could be siphoned off for use in the non-marketed sector; after 1960, they claimed, government had taken increasingly more of the marketed sector's production. Since Bacon and Eltis saw workers as able to pass on tax increases to profits they argued that the implication of this process was to reduce productive investment and thus long-run growth.[1]

Once again, subsequent research and experience make this hypothesis seem much less plausible now than it did at the time. There are two chief objections to the argument:

(i) In the long run the rise in government-financed non-marketed sector consumption has come not at the expense of marketed sector investment but rather has displaced marketed sector consumption—far more workers pay income tax (Crafts, 1991).

(ii) Although there was no decline in the relative size of the non-marketed sector in the 1980s, the profit squeeze evaporated and the share of profits in value-added returned to 1960s levels. Indeed, this would be predicted by standard models of the labour market in which normal profits—that is, a fairly constant mark-up of prices over costs—are achieved in equilibrium and real wages are adjusted to a level consistent with this by the pressure of unemployment (Layard *et al.*, 1991). In other words, we would expect the growth of the non-marketed sector to raise the *non-accelerating inflation rate of unemployment (NAIRU)** rather than affect investment or growth in the long run.

(iii) Kaldor's Formulation

One of the most influential items in the post-war debate on growth was Kaldor's inaugural lecture (1966). In it he drew attention to the apparent existence of a positive relationship which applied only in the manufacturing sector between growth

---

[1] In terms of equation (3), I_n and C_n grew at the expense of I_m.

$$Y_m - C_m = I_n + C_n + NX_m + I_m \qquad (3)$$

where the subscripts m and n refer to the marketed and non-marketed sectors.

of the workforce and increasing labour productivity.[1] In Kaldor's formulation this resulted from *dynamic economies of scale** and justified policies (such as the Selective Employment Tax) to shift employment from services to manufacturing.

Slow growth in Britain was seen as having resulted from the absence of a large pool of agricultural labour to draw on for the expansion of manufacturing employment. Moreover, a 'vicious circle' explanation of relative economic decline arises if Kaldor's hypothesis is linked to a balance-of-payments constraint in which slow growth retards productivity growth which in turn reduces the prospect of loosening the constraint, for example through increased competitiveness. The Kaldor hypothesis is thus consistent with the 'House of Lords view'.

Yet again, the evidence in favour of this analysis of growth is unpersuasive. Two pieces of evidence should be noted.

(i) Chatterji and Wickens (1983), who estimated *time-series** of equation (4) for six countries for 1960-80, found in only one case, the United States, that the growth of labour productivity in manufacturing (p_m) was positively related to the growth of manufacturing employment (l_m). In a more detailed study for aggregate UK manufacturing in the 1960s and 1970s the same authors (1982) found strong cyclical effects associated with varying labour utilisation rates (*Okun's Law** effects), but they econometrically rejected the hypothesis of dynamic economies of scale.

(ii) In a detailed *cross-sectional study** of British manufacturing during 1954-86, Oulton (1992) found that output growth is more strongly related to productivity growth in low- and negative-growth industries than in fast-growth industries which, as he remarks, is strong evidence against an interpretation based on productivity change in which increasing returns based on learning effects dominate.

In sum, the models reviewed in this sub-section provide little support for the view that growth rates of GDP are primarily a function of the size or rate of increase of the manufacturing base or the balance of manufacturing trade. Nor, incidentally, would

[1] Thus

$$p_m = a + bl_m \qquad (4)$$

where p_m is the rate of growth of output per worker in manufacturing, l_m is the rate of growth of employment in manufacturing and $b > 0$.

they account for the revival of UK productivity in the 1980s which is reviewed in detail in Section III.

'Catch-Up' and Convergence

A significant feature of long-run economic growth among OECD countries is the presence of processes of 'catch-up'. In general, the existence of a large productivity gap between any given country and the leader means there is potential for faster growth while catching up the leader. Allowance for 'catch-up' needs to be made, both when judging relative growth performance over time and when assessing future growth prospects (Dowrick and Nguyen, 1989). Thus, Table 5 implies that Britain had less scope for catch-up growth in the 1950s than France or Germany whereas the opposite was true by the 1980s. It also implies that, as happened in practice, European growth could be expected to fall considerably from the rapid rates of the early post-war period as catch-up was largely accomplished.

Table 11 seeks to quantify the 'catch-up' proposition and records results derived from regression analysis reported in Crafts (1992). The bonus from catch-up and reconstruction is an estimate of the normal benefit to be derived from the initial productivity gap. Three points should be noted.

(i)   The general slowdown of growth in the OECD owes a good deal to the exhaustion of catch-up opportunities and can therefore be expected to be long lasting. The unweighted average impact measured by the reduction in the bonus in Table 11 is about 1·4 percentage points per year over the 10-year period 1979-88 compared with the 1950s. Comparison of Table 11 with the growth accounting estimates of Table 3 demonstrates that this looms quite large relative to the slowdown of total factor productivity growth.

(ii) The Table confirms that in the 1950s both France and Germany had relatively large growth potential from catch-up; it also confirms the erosion by the 1980s of that potential. The bonus for Britain is noticeably less than that for Germany during the *Wirtschaftswunder* years. Thus normalising for differences in catch-up potential is clearly important in assessing growth rates.

(iii) Nevertheless, it is clear from Tables 3 and 11 that allowing for catch-up is not sufficient to explain slower British growth

[29]

TABLE 11

GROWTH RATE OF REAL GDP/HOUR WORKED: ACTUAL AND POTENTIAL BONUS FROM CATCH-UP AND RECONSTRUCTION

| | 1950-60 | | 1960-73 | | 1979-88 | |
	Actual	Bonus	Actual	Bonus	Actual	Bonus
Australia	2·9	1·2	2·5	0·5	0·8	0·4
Austria	5·9	2·8	5·9	1·3	1·5	0·5
Belgium	3·2	2·1	5·3	1·1	2·7	0·4
Canada	3·2	0·2	3·1	0·3	1·8	0·3
Denmark	3·1	1·9	5·2	1·1	1·0	0·6
Finland	4·1	2·4	5·9	1·4	3·5	0·7
France	4·5	2·1	5·5	1·0	3·2	0·3
Germany	7·0	2·9	5·3	1·0	2·2	0·3
Italy	4·2	2·4	6·4	1·2	2·2	0·4
Japan	5·8	4·0	9·9	2·2	3·5	0·9
Netherlands	4·1	1·9	4·6	0·8	2·6	0·2
Norway	4·0	1·8	4·2	0·9	2·5	0·4
Sweden	3·5	1·3	4·7	0·8	1·3	0·3
Switzerland	3·1	1·1	3·4	0·7	2·0	0·5
UK	**2·3**	**1·6**	**3·8**	**0·8**	**2·8**	**0·5**
USA	2·4	0·0	2·5	0·0	1·8	0·0

Source: Derived from Crafts (1992), see text; bonus calculated relative to USA in each period.

in the 1950s and 1960s. There were, evidently, other aspects of the economy leading to an inferior performance.

Countries differ in their ability to take advantage of catch-up possibilities. This may perhaps reflect different capabilities to achieve *technology transfer** associated with institutional arrangements in the context of technology policy (Ergas, 1987), training and/or industrial relations (Prais, 1981), in all of which Britain has been allegedly deficient.[1] Economic historians have

---

[1] But see J. R. Shackleton, *Training Too Much?*, subtitled 'A Sceptical Look at the Economics of Skill Provision in the UK', Hobart Paper No. 118, London: Institute of Economic Affairs, 1992, for a contrary view.

also emphasised the importance of political economy and self-interested behaviour. As Abramovitz puts it:

> 'Social capability [for catch-up] depends on more than the content of education and the organisation of firms ... it is a question of the obstacles to change raised by vested interests, established positions and customary relations among firms and between employers and employees' (1986, p. 389).

According to writers like Olson (1982), these obstacles to change in democratic European countries tended to intensify as the post-war period progressed, leading to 'Eurosclerosis' and the withering away of growth potential.

The Role of Convergence in Growth

The importance of catch-up in the comparative growth process leaves open some very important issues relating to convergence. In traditional neo-classical models of economic growth, the sources of growth equation (1) would result from a 'well-behaved' production function.[1] If resources are efficiently allocated, then in the long run total factor productivity grows through technological progress which is regarded as exogenous and freely available to all countries. Diminishing returns to capital accumulation ensure that the investment rate has no effect on the steady-state growth rate. Output per person depends on savings rates relative to population growth which will influence the capital-intensity of the economy; if these rates are the same, closed economies will converge to the same income and output per person. The speed of convergence depends on returns to capital and savings rates. In open economies the process can be complicated by the migration of factors of production and/or delays in the diffusion of technology, but the same eventual outcome is predicted.

Whether the insights of this *heuristic model** are valid in the real world is a question which underlies most recent research on growth, both statistical and theoretical. Empirically, Barro and Martin (1991) find evidence of underlying convergence within the advanced world averaging about 2 per cent per year. Nevertheless, Table 12 indicates that their traditional neo-classical

---

[1] For example,

$$Y = AK^{\alpha} L^{\beta} \qquad (5)$$

where $\alpha + \beta = 1$, $0 < \alpha$, $\beta < 1$ and A represents the total factor productivity of the economy.

TABLE 12

ACTUAL AND FORECAST CONVERGENCE, 1950-1986/87

	GDP/Hour Worked (USA = 100)		TFP Growth (% p.a.)	Equipment Investment (% GDP)	Lawyers/ Doctors
	Actual	Forecast			
(a) *OECD Countries*					
Australia	78	81	1·9	na	0·27
Austria	74	43	2·1	9·91	0·12
Belgium	86	60	2·4	6·84	0·50
Canada	92	86	1·2	7·71	0·92
Denmark	68	61	1·8	6·88	0·28
Finland	67	48	2·9	12·06	0·97
France	94	58	2·7	8·79	0·30
Germany	80	47	1·9	8·90	0·32
Italy	79	48	2·9	6·83	0·28
Japan	61	27	3·9	12·23	0·09
Netherlands	92	64	2·1	7·78	0·15
Norway	90	61	2·0	7·01	0·27
Sweden	82	67	1·5	na	na
Switzerland	68	72	0·6	na	0·21
UK	**80**	**73**	**1·7**	**6·94**	**0·62**
(b) *Developing Countries*					
Argentina	28	50	0·4	2·14	0·78
Brazil	25	29	0·8	6·46	na
Chile	33	53	0·8	1·54	2·14
Colombia	28	38	na	2·29	na
India	4	8	0·1	2·78	1.23
Korea	21	18	2·4	5·57	na
Mexico	27	35	1·1	2·73	na
Peru	20	34	na	2·67	na
Phillipines	11	20	na	4·45	na
Taiwan	20	15	2·8	na	na

Notes and Sources: Actual GDP/hour worked: Maddison (1989) (1991); Forecast GDP/ hour worked is based on Barro and Martin (1991); for full details see Crafts (1992).

[32]

model has not predicted post-war convergence tendencies very precisely and suggests that convergence rates differ substantially. Regression analysis suggests that higher investment in equipment does speed up convergence but a higher lawyer/doctor ratio slows it down (Crafts, 1992). The lawyer/doctor ratio reflects the allocation of talent in the economy; a large share of human capital deployed in the legal profession suggests that able people find it more attractive to seek rents than to create wealth. This in turn reflects incentive problems associated with institutional arrangements inimical to growth.

More sophisticated econometric analysis of the growth of GDP per person suggests that there is convergence within different groups of countries but not between them; that is to say, there is evidence of local convergence without full global convergence (Durlauf and Johnson, 1992). Two questions naturally arise from such a finding. Does it also apply to sectors such as manufacturing? What determines to which club a country belongs?

Let us consider again Table 6 (above, p. 19). Broadberry (1992b) suggests that there is a large and persistent gap in labour productivity between European countries which belong to one convergence club and the United States. Research on the pre-Second World War period suggests this may result from the importance of different natural resource endowments given the technology of the time (Nelson and Wright, 1992), and perhaps from differences in the acceptability of corporate capitalism (Chandler, 1990) and of management/union control of the shopfloor (Tolliday and Zeitlin, 1991). None of these arguments holds much sway now, however. Yet, in the recent past, while Japan has continued to narrow the productivity gap with the United States (Pilat and Van Ark, 1991), Germany has ceased to do so. Further exploration of these issues is fundamental to the prospects of productivity growth in the future.

New Growth Economics

A common theme in the *new growth economics**, in contrast with the traditional approach, is to examine neo-classical models in which the growth rate is an endogenous outcome of investments of various kinds and in which persistent differences in growth between countries can result. Models of this kind stress the importance of *externalities**, envisage more scope for structural differences to affect long-run growth, are more conducive to failures of global convergence, and permit more potential for government policy to change growth rates. They may come closer to upholding the essence of the 'House of Lords View'. At the same time, they are largely unproven empirically. A good diagrammatic exposition can be found in Van de Klundert and Smulders (1992).

The Romer Approach

Early work in this area followed Romer (1986).[1] This supposed that the impact of capital investment on output is much bigger than assumed by conventional growth accounting which infers the impact from the share of profits in income. In fact, Romer argued that, once all the external effects of investment not reflected in private profits are taken into account, investment may not be subject to diminishing returns but to constant returns. Thus faster capital stock growth has a *pro rata* effect on growth and (where $\alpha + \gamma = 1$) increases in investment will have permanent growth rate effects. Moreover, since the rate of growth of the capital stock is the investment rate divided by the capital to output ratio, anything which raises the productivity of capital will also have permanent growth rate effects, as Baldwin (1989) pointed out in an analysis of the EC Single Market (1992) initiative.

Nevertheless, there is evidence that the external effects of investment are small. Crafts (1992) reviewed the available evidence and reached that conclusion.[2] Crafts's conclusion is supported by detailed econometric investigations of post-war British manufacturing by Oulton (1992) and O'Mahoney (1992a); they both concluded that they could not reject the hypothesis that $\gamma = 0$. Thus it is most likely that the spillover effects of investment are small and that there are diminishing returns to capital formation. Indeed, in this respect the analysis provided by growth accounting of the rôle of investment in growth may be reasonably accurate.

More recent vintages of *endogenous growth models** have abandoned the Romer (1986) approach and, in various ways,

---

[1] This can be represented as proposing a production function of the following kind:

$$Y = AK^{\alpha + \gamma} L^{\beta} \tag{6}$$

where the addition to the conventional exponent on capital represents externalities to capital formation including learning effects, spillovers, etc. The growth accounting exercise of Table 3 implicitly assumes $\gamma = 0$.

[2] More precisely, Crafts's conclusion is that $\alpha + \gamma < 1$, with γ probably quite small.

stress the rôle of human capital. In the traditional model this would be seen simply as augmenting the rate of growth of the labour force through improvement of its quality; Maddison treats human capital in precisely this way in the estimates in Table 3 (above, p. 15). But Lucas (1988), in a seminal contribution, suggested a fundamentally different approach.

The Lucas Model

The Lucas model proposes additional, external effects of human capital on output: human capital embodied in a worker raises the productivity of colleagues.[1] It is assumed that a constant rate of growth of human capital results from devoting a constant share of the population's time to education as knowledge passes from generation to generation. Policy interventions to raise the amount of education will have a permanent growth rate effect in this model and these externalities provide a way for growth rates permanently to differ between countries unmitigated by market forces.

There appear to have been only two attempts so far to estimate the Lucas effect. Rauch (1991) found that the net external effect of a year's extra schooling raises the level of TFP by 2·8 per cent. Average years of schooling in OECD countries have risen by about five years since 1913 and at very similar rates (Maddison, 1991, Table 3.8). If Rauch's estimate is reliable, the Lucas effect does not go very far to explain observed total factor productivity growth or account for differences in growth rates within the OECD. O'Mahony (1992a) finds only weak evidence of Lucas effects in German and British manufacturing. Her results do suggest, however, that while the allowances made for education effects by Maddison (1991) are of the right order of magnitude, it is important to build up more data on magnitudes of skill formation other than simply years of schooling. Indeed, neither these investigations nor that of the Romer (1986) model suggest for the time being the necessity seriously to modify any of the conclusions on the sources of growth drawn earlier from Table 3.

More directly addressing the notion that manufacturing matters for growth is a second model proposed in the same paper by Lucas (1988), building on earlier work by Krugman (1987). Here human capital is accumulated through work

[1] The simplest way to think of this is to return to equation (1) and regard the term ΔTFP/TFP as representing these externalities from the growth of human capital.

The Krugman-Lucas Model

Figure 1, derived from Krugman (1987), extends this model into a many goods, Ricardian model of international trade. This diagram shows the simultaneous determination of the pattern of specialisation and relative wages. Goods are cheaper to produce if relative wages are less than the ratio of the home country's productivity to that abroad—the margin of specialisation as relative wages change is shown by the AA curve. The more

Figure 1:
Short- and Long-Run Specialisation in International Trade

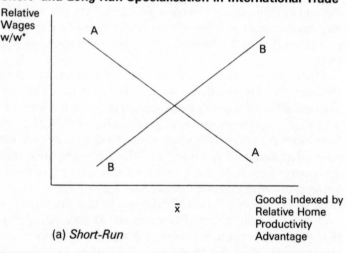

(a) *Short-Run*

experience which reduces the unit labour requirement over time but at rates which differ between sectors. Thus an economy's initial comparative advantage determines future growth rates. If specialisation is in activities which have high learning effects, then living standards improve relatively quickly. Moreover, this learning will tend to reinforce the initial pattern of comparative advantage.[1]

---

[1] Lucas considers a simple two-good case where output is determined as follows:

$$Y_1 = h_1 u_1 L_1 \qquad (7a)$$
$$Y_2 = h_2 u_2 L_2 \qquad (7b)$$

[*Cont'd. on p. 37*]

goods are produced at home the higher is the relative demand for home labour and thus the ratio w/w* shown by the BB curve. Equilibrium in Figure 1(a) is where the curves intersect and goods to the left of this point are produced domestically. Once the pattern of specialisation is established, changes in relative productivity reinforce the position and in the long run the AA curve will become vertical around the original intersection within limits set by competitiveness without experience, as shown in Figure 1(b). Specialisation in a subset of manufacturing with higher learning by doing will then imply permanently faster growth.

Figure 1 (continued):

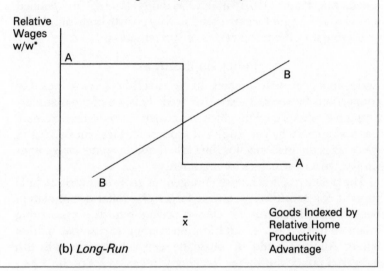

(b) *Long-Run*

The Krugman/Lucas model (see Box 1) clearly permits scope for policy-makers to influence growth rates since, within limits, they can act to shift comparative advantage through protectionist

where h is human capital and u is the fraction of the workforce in the sector while

$$h_i = h_i \delta_i u_i \qquad (8)$$

that is, human capital growth depends on learning by doing. Assume $\delta 1 > \delta 2$.

If there is complete specialisation along the lines of comparative advantage, growth rates will be $\delta 1$ and (measured in terms of good 1 as numeraire) $\delta 2 + \Delta TT/TT$, where TT is the relative price of good 2 over good 1. Provided these goods are relatively close substitutes, the country which specialises in good 1 will have permanently faster growth. Given a learning technology like (8), skill accumulation intensifies original comparative advantage.

[37]

infant industry policies. Also shocks to the country's balance-of-payments position which shift the equilibrium specialisation[1] can have long-run growth effects. House of Lords (1985) seems to have had such a model in mind in the context of its fears about the long-term implications of North Sea oil and early-1980s monetarism.

Nevertheless, despite its intellectual appeal, there is as yet little empirical evidence to suggest that the Krugman/Lucas model is generally a good way of explaining why growth rates differ or of obtaining powerful insights for policy formulation. Indeed, recent British experience seems to argue the other way. Not only does Oulton's (1992) econometric study find against strong learning effects in relative UK sectoral productivity growth, as already noted, but Panic (1976) and O'Mahony (1992b) in detailed overviews of Anglo-German productivity growth both found little or no rôle for different patterns of specialisation.

Policy Implications

Endogenous growth models have established some possible connections between the size and trade balance of the manufacturing sector and growth which are absent in the traditional neo-classical approach. Yet empirical support for these models is still weak, as is the evidence for the earlier, and in some ways rather similar, macro-structuralist arguments.

The policy implications of endogenous growth models include support for subsidising various forms of capital accumulation because social returns will exceed private returns, for pursuing infant industry policies and for intervening to combat market failure. All these could, of course, be seen as hallmarks of British industrial policy during the 'picking winners' years of the 1960s and 1970s when relative economic decline was at its most virulent.

Before accepting these nostrums it would seem sensible to consider more carefully institutional aspects of differences in success at catch-up in post-war growth. The question may perhaps be asked: Should more attention be given to incentives and political economy and rather less to learning effects and investment?

[1] In terms of Figure 1 such shocks would shift the BB curve.

III. BRITISH ECONOMIC GROWTH BEFORE
AND AFTER 1979

It is now time to review Britain's growth record more closely in order to throw more light on the theoretical arguments discussed above but, more importantly, to permit an assessment of changing government policy and to highlight key aspects of the rôle of the supply-side in the growth process. Growth performance since the 'Thatcher Revolution' is set in an historical and institutional context.

Was Growth Performance Better in the 1980s?

Conservative administrations in the 1980s pursued a series of supply-side policy reforms which departed radically from all previous post-war approaches to the pursuit of faster growth. This sub-section provides some initial data on the growth record for the 1979-89 business cycle in relation to those of earlier comparable periods.

Table 13 reports productivity growth trends for the business sector of OECD economies—the government sector is omitted to reduce measurement difficulties. This evidence suggests there was a distinct improvement in the UK's relative performance in the 1980s but that the rate of productivity growth stayed below that of the 1960s and there was no Japanese-style miracle. *Prima facie*, there are grounds for regarding this performance as an improvement, but three questions have to be examined before such a judgement can be confirmed.

(i) How does UK performance look when normalised for the differential effects of the potential for 'catching-up' discussed in Section II?

(ii) Does any improvement also show up in terms of wider measures of economic welfare?

(iii) Are there implications for future performance which need also to be taken into account?

The first two of these issues are tackled here while the third is held over to later in the section.

[39]

TABLE 13

PRODUCTIVITY IN THE BUSINESS SECTOR, 1960-1989

(annual average compound growth rates)
(per cent)

	Total Factor Productivity			Labour Productivity		
	1960-73	1973-79	1979-89	1960-73	1973-79	1979-89
United States	1·6	−0·4	0·4	2·2	0·0	0·8
Japan	5·9	1·4	2·0	8·6	2·9	3·0
Germany	2·8	1·8	0·8	4·5	3·1	1·6
France	4·0	1·7	1·7	5·4	3·0	2·6
Italy	4·6	2·2	1·3	6·3	2·9	2·1
UK	**2·3**	**0·6**	**1·5**	**3·6**	**1·6**	**2·1**
Canada	2·0	0·8	0·4	2·8	1·5	1·4
Austria	3·4	1·2	0·8	5·8	3·2	2·0
Belgium	3·9	1·5	1·4	5·2	2·8	2·4
Denmark	2·8	1·2	1·3	4·3	2·6	2·1
Finland	3·3	1·5	2·7	5·0	3·2	3·8
Greece	5·8	1·5	−0·3	8·8	3·3	0·4
Netherlands	3·1	1·5	0·8	4·8	2·8	1·5
Norway	2·4	−0·7	−0·2	4·0	0·3	0·6
Spain	4·1	1·4	2·1	6·0	3·5	3·3
Sweden	2·7	0·4	1·0	4·1	1·5	1·7
Switzerland	2·0	−0·4	0·9	3·2	0·7	1·6
Australia	1·7	0·9	0·6	2·7	2·2	1·1
New Zealand	0·9	−1·8	0·9	1·6	−1·2	1·8
OECD Europe	3·4	1·4	1·3	5·0	2·6	2·1
OECD	2·8	0·5	0·9	4·1	1·4	1·6

Source: OECD (1991c).

Table 14 is based on the same regression used in preparing Table 11. Growth in a cross-section of OECD countries was analysed explicitly to isolate the effects of catch-up on total factor productivity growth. Table 14 reveals whether countries grew faster (+) or slower (−) than one would have expected after allowing for the growth of factors of production and initial

TABLE 14

REGRESSION ESTIMATES OF 'RESIDUAL GROWTH'

(per cent per year)

	1950-60	*1960-73*	*1979-88*
Australia	−0·43	−1·58	−1·28
Austria	0·98	−0·02	−0·92
Belgium	−0·66	0·31	0·80
Canada	0·96	0·33	0·05
Denmark	−1·41	0·09	−0·92
Finland	−0·72	0·16	0·73
France	0·19	0·58	1·10
Germany	1·97	−0·34	0·09
Italy	0·16	0·83	0·07
Japan	0·37	2·17	0·16
Netherlands	−0·16	−0·33	0·58
Norway	−1·30	−0·93	0·03
Sweden	0·05	0·33	−0·30
Switzerland	0·10	−1·04	−0·57
UK	**−0·80**	**−0·63**	**0·84**
USA	0·69	0·07	0·26

Source: Crafts (1992).

productivity gaps. The UK is seen to have 'underperformed' by
an average of about 0·7 per cent per year in the 1950s and 1960s
but to have bounced back in the 1980s when 'overperforming'
by 0·8 per cent for a net improvement of 1·5 (= 0·7 + 0·8) per
cent per year. Interestingly, despite the praise often heaped on
Germany by foreigners, performance there seems to have gone
in the opposite direction.

'Measurable Economic Welfare'

An answer to the second of these questions can be obtained
using Table 15 which is based on the methodology of a famous
work by Nordhaus and Tobin (1972), as modified by Beckerman
(1980). 'Measurable economic welfare' (MEW) adapts GDP
growth estimates to allow for changes in leisure time and income

TABLE 15

GROWTH OF MEASURABLE ECONOMIC WELFARE/HEAD, 1950-73 AND 1979-89

(per cent per year)

	(a) Real GDP/ Head	(b) Leisure Imputed	(c) Inequality Adjustment	(d) MEW/ Head
(a) 1950-73				
Belgium	3·6	−0·1	na	3·5
Denmark	3·5	0·2	na	3·7
France	4·3	−0·2	1·1	5·2
Germany	4·6	0·1	0·1	4·8
Italy	4·6	2·7	na	7·3
Netherlands	na	na	na	na
UK	**2·4**	**−0·6**	**−0·1**	**1·7**
(b) 1979-89				
Belgium	1·9	1·2	na	3·1
Denmark	1·8	−0·2	na	1·6
France	1·6	1·1	na	2·7
Germany	1·7	0·3	na	2·0
Italy	2·3	0·3	na	2·6
Netherlands	1·0	0·9	na	1·9
UK	**2·1**	**0·5**	**−0·6**	**2·0**

Source: Based on Crafts (1993) which contains further detailed sources and methods.

distribution. Additional leisure is generally regarded as a good and to some extent greater productive potential may be used to reduce work effort as well as to produce and consume more output. (The valuation of this extra leisure has, however, been controversial.) Many economists would see rising income inequality as undesirable, although how far, if at all, this should detract from the welfare gains from faster growth is very much a value-judgement. Beckerman's approach uses the *Atkinson index of inequality** which allows (indeed requires) the analyst explicitly to choose a trade-off between the distribution and size of GDP.

Table 15 shows some illustrative calculations for the growth of MEW. There was a sharp increase in inequality in Britain between the mid-1970s and mid-1980s such that the bottom 20 per cent of households saw virtually no gain in real income and the proportion below the 'poverty line' approximately doubled (Jenkins, 1991).[1] Most of this rise can be attributed to the 'Thatcher Experiment' (Johnson and Webb, 1992). Inequality data are not yet available for other EC countries, but comparisons of estimated trends in poverty suggest that the UK was exceptional (O'Higgins and Jenkins, 1990) and that any adjustments eventually inserted in column (c) would be likely to be very small. Big changes in hours worked per year and female labour force participation rates, which have varied substantially between countries, are also reflected in Table 15. The main points that arise from this Table are:

o In the recent period, rankings of growth performance are much more sensitive to imputations for leisure and inequality than in the 1950s and 1960s.

o Although in general the estimated slowdown in growth of MEW since the 1960s is similar to that of GDP, on these assumptions the UK had higher growth of MEW in 1979-89 than in 1950-73 (though its GDP growth rate was lower).

o In the Thatcher period there are two generally offsetting and large imputations for the UK—a positive leisure component and a negative inequality one. In these calculations they virtually cancel out, but with different assumptions about the value of leisure or a different degree of dislike for inequality this need not be the case.

o Nevertheless, experiments with a range of assumptions do suggest that most economists compiling an estimate of MEW would conclude that the UK's improvement relative to Europe since the 1960s has been appreciable.

All in all, it seems probable that Britain's growth performance relative both to other countries and to underlying potential improved distinctly during the 1980s. Raw GDP data give a misleading impression of the achievements of the 1950s and 1960s compared with more recent times.

---

1 This concept of 'poverty line' is a relativist one and thus reflects changes in income distributions rather than absolute levels of consumption; poverty is defined as having less than half average 'equivalent income'. 'Equivalent income' is income by household normalised for composition of household membership.

Slow Growth in the 'Golden Age', 1950-73

Tables 3, 11 and 14 suggest that relatively slow growth in the UK in the long, pre-OPEC post-war boom (often referred to as the *'Golden Age'**) was primarily due to weak growth of total factor productivity. Moreover, this resulted only partly from lower catch-up possibilities and represented a distinctly below-par performance. Let us now probe deeper into the reasons for this under-achievement, in particular by drawing contrasts with West Germany which is typically seen as much more successful in this period.

Germany had more rapid accumulation of capital of various kinds than the UK which contributed to faster growth with some effect on measured TFP growth. In turn, this was influenced by persistent institutional differences. Nevertheless, it seems unlikely that new growth economics can explain anything like the whole of the gap in growth rates.

De Long and Summers (1991) have put forward the strongest quantitative evidence to suggest that physical investment (especially in equipment) has big positive externalities. However, accepting their estimated coefficient, which is probably much too high (Oulton, 1992), would account for only a little under 0·5 percentage points of the growth rate gap.

Role of 'Long-termist' Investments in Germany

Germany may have derived some benefits from its greater propensity to undertake 'long-termist' investments involving accrual of knowledge, although years of schooling of the labour force (Maddison, 1991) and total expenditure on R+D (Englander and Mittelstadt, 1988) were at this point very much the same as for Britain. A number of writers (for example, Franks and Mayer, 1990) have emphasised the difference in capital markets in encouraging German firms, free from threats of hostile takeover, to take a longer-term view of investment.

Germany was notably more successful in producing patented results from its technological activities—it accounted for a similar fraction of patents in the United States in the mid-1950s but double the UK share by the mid-1970s (Pavitt and Soete, 1982). Econometric estimates by Englander and Mittelstadt (1988) indicate that the faster growth of the stock of R+D output may have accounted for about 0·3 percentage points difference in growth rates.

Traditionally, more German workers acquired formal vocational qualifications—by 1979, 61 per cent of German workers compared with 23 per cent of UK workers (Steedman, 1990). There was already a much greater emphasis on vocational training in Germany before the war (Barnett, 1986, pp. 201-33). There exists no estimate of the impact of this greater training on growth. However, O'Mahony (1992b) found that human capital accounted for a 12 percentage point gap between British and German manufacturing productivity in 1987. Much of this may come from externalities (O'Mahony, 1992a). Using the same methodology, Crafts (1993) put human capital's impact in 1979 at 14 percentage points. If this had all built up since 1950, it would explain about 0·4 per cent per year slower growth in the UK but, given the long-standing training gap, it seems likely that the effect would be much smaller.

The evidence therefore suggests that a third or perhaps even a half of the gap between German and British growth cannot be explained by new growth economics. There remains a gap in TFP growth to be accounted for, so it is important also to look at the efficiency with which factors of production were used (rather than simply the rate at which they were accumulated).

'Behavioural Differences'

Pratten's study of multinational companies finds that 'behavioural differences' resulting from management-union interactions were responsible for about half the observed productivity gap in the early 1970s (Table 16). The finding on behavioural factors is consistent with the outcome of 25 studies for various times in the post-war period listed by Pratten and Atkinson (1976, p. 574), 23 of which report inefficient labour usage. There seems to have been an impact on the growth of productivity, not simply on the level; for example, Prais (1981) documented the retarding effects of negotiating appropriate manning levels in the 1960s and 1970s, when new technology came along in six out of 10 industrial case studies he undertook (brewing, tobacco, motor vehicles, tyres, metal boxes and newspapers).

Behavioural differences which impinge on productivity outcomes are shaped by institutions and market forces which influence bargaining power—between firms and their workers and between government and industry—in a world often characterised by imperfect and indeed asymmetric information. Industrial relations and 'competition policy' are therefore both worth close attention.

TABLE 16

LABOUR PRODUCTIVITY COMPARISONS IN
INTERNATIONAL COMPANIES: REASONS FOR
PRODUCTIVITY DIFFERENTIALS, 1972

	German Advantage Over UK (%)	North American Advantage Over UK (%)
'Economic' Causes		
Length of Production Runs	5½	20½
Plant and Machinery	5	6
Other[a]	2	6
'Behavioural' Causes		
Strikes and Restrictive Practices	3½	5
Manning and Efficiency	8½	6
Total Differential[b]	27	50

Notes:

[a] Other economic causes include differences in product mix, capacity utilisation, and quality of materials.

[b] The contributions to the total differential are multiplicative, not additive.

Source: Pratten (1976).

Formal economic analysis predicts that the multi-unionism characteristic of Britain but not of Germany in this period will tend to produce bargains with lower levels of effort and/or greater overmanning (Machin and Wadhwani, 1989): these predictions are supported by Anglo-German experience (Flanagan *et al.*, 1983). However, the conduct of industrial relations and resulting bargaining equilibria will depend especially on the slackness of the labour market facing a union, the degree of competition facing a firm, and the risk of a firm's going bankrupt. Such factors were all much more conducive to low productivity outcomes in the full employment years 1950-73 than in the 1980s.

'Competition Policy'

'Competition policy' must be considered in a rather wider sense than simply anti-trust legislation, as Olson's (1982) work suggests. More important is the extent to which both private and nationalised producers are sheltered from market forces through protectionism or soft budget constraints (where bankruptcy is averted by the availability of extra government funds). The ability of government to make credible commitments to strict policy rules precluding discretionary subsidy will affect the amount of resources devoted to lobbying and both the speed and the extent of adjustment to an efficient allocation of resources as circumstances change (Rodrik, 1990). Recognising these arguments makes the case for subsidising investment much more doubtful than new growth theory suggests or was generally thought in the 1950s to 1970s. The question that has to be answered is whether any externalities are sufficient to outweigh the inducements to less efficient use of factors of production.

Morris and Stout characterised the basis of UK industrial policy in the period 1945-72 as 'investment-led growth', with a heavy emphasis on public subsidies to capital accumulation (1985, p. 862). In manufacturing, investment as a share of output during the 1960s and 1970s was very similar to that in Germany (Hill, 1979) but the productivity of German investment was almost twice as great (CBI, 1977). Ulman observed that

'overmanning by international standards occurs in the most modern docks, printing plants, steel mills, and transportation equipment, to cite a few prominent examples' (1968, p. 337).

Hitchens *et al.* (1990) found that in Northern Ireland, where capital subsidies in 1979 were 22 per cent of manufacturing GDP compared with 2·3 per cent in Britain and investment per employee was 10 per cent higher, the main result was to allow management to continue overmanning. Northern Ireland's productivity is 20 per cent lower and has not been converging to the British level. Sargent and Scott (1986) document the serious allocative distortions in investment decisions resulting from the tax and subsidy system. Thus, it seems improbable that subsidising investment did much in practice to accelerate growth.

Weakness in British Nationalised Industries

The consequences for bargained productivity outcomes of soft budget constraints and lack of competition were most vividly seen in the British nationalised industries which accounted for about 20 per cent of all investment. Vickers and Yarrow (1988) point to major problems resulting from lax government control

TABLE 17
PRODUCTIVITY OUTCOMES IN
UK NATIONALISED/PRIVATISED SECTOR

	Labour Productivity Growth (% per annum)		Mid-1970s Relative Labour Productivity Level	
	1968-78	1979-88	WG/UK	USA/UK
Coal	−0·7	6·2	2·64	7·60
Railways	0·8	0·8	1·08	3·95
Steel	−0·2	9·4	1·52	2·57
Electricity	5·3	3·2	2·25	3·47
Postal	−1·3	2·2	1·07	2·28
Gas	8·5	5·2	2·23	2·79
Telecom	8·2	5·6	1·07	2·69
Airways	6·4	4·2	1·59	1·52
Nat. Freight	2·7	3·7	1·27	1·80

Sources: Productivity growth, 1968-78 (Pryke, 1981); productivity growth, 1979-88 (Bishop and Kay, 1988); productivity levels (Smith *et al.*, 1982).

in which politicians' incentives were to condone and conceal overmanning and overinvestment. Reports by the Monopolies and Mergers Commission in the early 1980s were severely critical of long records of misuse of manpower and capital in both coal (MMC, 1983) and electricity (MMC, 1981). Table 17 confirms the poor productivity performance of the 1970s and shows the improvements of the 1980s. Then, in the still nationalised coal and steel sectors, government reformed productivity by putting itself in the new position of accepting plant closures, setting credible financial targets and acting to enhance its bargaining power *vis-à-vis* both management and unions.

Successive governments sought co-operation with the TUC and placed a high priority on saving jobs, especially in the regions. Perhaps it is not therefore surprising to find Silberston's assessment of the industrial policies of the 1960s and 1970s as 'directed at helping old industries to survive rather than encouraging new products and new technology' (1981, p. 49). The early post-war years were a period in which import penetration was low and many industries were collusive (Gribbin, 1978). Moreover, although hostile takeovers emerged as a threat to sleepy management, the evidence strongly suggests that the merger and takeover boom of the 1960s did little in practice to raise productivity growth or discriminate effectively against the incompetent manager (Cowling *et al.*, 1980; Meeks, 1977; Singh, 1975).

In sum, the evidence is that a good deal of the relatively slow growth of the UK during the 'Golden Age' was due to an environment which permitted or even encouraged the survival of the inefficient and created a situation where the bargaining power of those seeking to block productivity-enhancing change was often considerable. Britain's less rapid catching-up of the United States reflects institutional differences. New growth economics offers insights into but by no means a full account of the growth gap between the UK and Germany while its apparent policy prescription of subsidy to investment is seen to have been unhelpful.

A Renaissance in the 1980s?

If the preceding account is correct, it implies that a policy configuration which changed bargaining power through raising unemployment, increasing competition and making firms' budget constraints tighter and harder would potentially have a substantial impact on productivity growth, at least during a transitional period until a new equilibrium was established. The change in policy régime and external shocks of the early 1980s provided a new economic environment along these lines.

In terms of reversing relative economic decline, the Thatcher programme of reforms entailed tax reform, privatisation, deregulation, harsh treatment of 'lame ducks', trade union reform, and a general distrust of public sector interventions to correct market failure. Trade union inputs into policy-making effectively ceased. The new policy stance affected the framework in which investment decisions and bargains between management and their workers were made, as well as having direct effects on the use of capital and labour. The thrust of policy was to attack restrictive practices and overmanning rather than to aim for investment-led growth. The high initial unemployment resulting from this strategy, coupled with a determined attempt to impose strict monetary discipline and a *petro-currency**, was accepted by the government without a Heath-style U-turn, although not fully anticipated.

[49]

Table 6 demonstrated the rapid reduction of the productivity gap between British and German manufacturing between 1979 and 1987. It is widely agreed that, at least until 1985, this recovery owed little or nothing to investment in people, plant or technology but came from more efficient use of existing factors of production. Recent econometric studies strongly support explanations based on the bargaining model of productivity. The 1980s initially saw a change in the conduct rather than the structure of industrial relations, with changed working practices and manning levels contingent on reduced trade union bargaining power which resulted both from unemployment shocks and greater competition in product markets (Bean and Symons, 1989; Haskel, 1991; Machin and Wadhwani, 1989). Notably, it is claimed that

'it is undeniable that the most dramatic changes in working practices have been achieved in industries with product market crises' (Brown and Wadhwani, 1990, p. 68).

It appears then that, in the 1980s, the UK performed a somewhat belated catching-up exercise associated with the switch in policy régime. The experience of this period serves to confirm the diagnosis that slow growth in the 'Golden Age' owed a good deal to institutional factors which served to reduce total factor productivity growth and which were politically very difficult to reform once entrenched in the economy.

British Technology Weakness Continues

By contrast, relative British weakness in technology and in accumulating capital, both human and physical, continued through the 1980s. The route to faster growth was not apparently the one prescribed by new growth economics. A recent assessment of technological capabilities which reviewed in-house expertise, managerial skills and commitment to particular technologies concluded that the UK remained a weak performer with a myopic system (Patel and Pavitt, 1988). Spending on R+D by industry lagged behind that in other countries—1·6 per cent of industrial GDP in 1988 compared with 2·2 per cent in Germany and 2·1 per cent in Japan (Stoneman, 1991, p. 12), while the British share of patents granted in the United States fell from 10·8 per cent in 1979 to 8·1 per cent in 1988 (OECD, 1991b, Table 21). Physical investment as a share of GDP was about 1 percentage point lower than in the 'Golden Age' (OECD, 1991a).

[50]

Assessments of training provision in Britain still remain fiercely critical despite increasing expenditure during the 1980s (Greenhalgh and Mavrotas, 1991; Marsden and Ryan, 1991). The proportion of workers with intermediate vocational qualifications increased only slightly (Steedman, 1990) and training expenditures as a share of labour costs remained lower than in Germany (OECD, 1991c). A production-function-based analysis of the impact of increased workforce skills in reducing the Anglo-German manufacturing productivity gap between 1979 and 1987 suggests a contribution of only 2 percentage points (Crafts, 1993). It should be remembered, however, that this does not necessarily imply that government should spend more. There are clearly potential dangers of an overspend here (Shackleton, 1992). Nevertheless, British institutional arrangements seem less conducive to investment in training than those elsewhere and this is a cause for concern.

The implications of these developments for future growth performance are ambiguous. Clearly, a good part of the better growth of the 1980s took the form of a once-and-for-all catch-up effect which will tend to peter out. It does not seem to be valid to invoke the Romer (1986) new growth model to suggest permanent growth-rate effects through a new constant higher output to capital ratio. Nor does it seem very promising to hope for a big increase in trend growth from improved human capital formation as in Lucas (1988) or Romer (1990).

No Return to the 1970s

Nevertheless, an early return to the policy approach and weak performance of the 1970s seems unlikely, given that we can expect the bargaining framework in which firms and unions operate to be set by pre-committed policy in the competitive environment of the Single Market and by fairly high unemployment. Moreover, by the end of the 1980s, changes in the structure of industrial relations consolidating the loss of trade union power were evident (Gregg, Machin and Metcalf, 1991; Purcell, 1991). There is therefore no reason to anticipate a slow productivity growth phase resulting from a lapse back to less favourable bargaining equilibria. Also, the gains from future technological improvements are less likely to be diluted than in the past by restrictive practices, so there should be some permanent effect on the growth rate.

Despite some unfortunate policy omissions, the Thatcher

period seems to have had important positive impacts on growth in the short term, which were obtained by changing bargaining power and by recognising the importance of incentive structures in productivity outcomes. As a result, some of the earlier obstacles to faster growth were removed or at least diminished. Moreover, thus far, this overview at the aggregate level suggests that although growth in the 1990s will probably not maintain the rates of the 1980s, a return to the behavioural problems contributing to the 'underperformance' of the 'Golden Age' (Table 14) can probably be avoided. Nevertheless, it is by no means clear that this will be sufficient to prevent a resumption of relative economic decline, given Britain's poor record in technology and human capital formation. Does this interim judgement require revision, however, when de-industrialisation is explicitly considered?

IV. DOES DE-INDUSTRIALISATION JEOPARDISE FUTURE GROWTH PROSPECTS?

The starting point of Section I was the 'House of Lords View' that future growth is threatened by a dangerous contraction of the manufacturing base and, especially, the weak balance of trade in manufactures which emerged during the 1980s. Two specific models were identified which might justify this claim, namely the balance-of-payments constraint model of Thirlwall (1979) and the Lucas (1988) extension of the Krugman model. It was also recognised that endogenous growth models might in general be used to support such arguments if externalities to factor accumulation were affected by declines in manufacturing. A *prima facie* review of the evidence in Section II suggested that the evidence in favour of any of these models was, however, rather slim.

Closer examination of the empirical content of the 'House of Lords View' is now required to consider whether Section III's provisional view of future growth prospects is sustainable or if, in the light of recent de-industrialisation, a gloomier view is appropriate. In particular, an interpretation of the changing balance-of-payments position of the 1980s is required in order to consider past and possible future changes in the terms of trade, and to explore at a disaggregated level the rôles of learning effects, external economies and industrial structure in productivity change.

Recent Developments in Britain's External Trade and Payments Position

Table 10 (above, p. 23) reported a striking change in Britain's trade position during the 1980s such that by 1989 there was a deficit on manufacturing trade amounting to 3·6 per cent of GDP. The current account of the balance of payments was about £20 billion in deficit in 1989 and even in 1991, a year of deep recession, the deficit was still about £5 billion, although as recently as 1985-86 it had been in surplus. Three questions arise:

(i) Does the UK's poor balance-of-payments performance

[53]

mean that the 1980s improvement in growth performance highlighted in Section III was somehow illusory?

(ii) What are the implications for the future equilibrium value of the pound and the terms of trade?

(iii) Should we now worry about a balance-of-payments constraint on growth?

The first two of these topics are dealt with in this sub-section while the third is the subject of the next sub-section. It should be noted that, although the trends revealed by these statistics are probably correct, there are unresolved problems concerning serious errors and omissions in world, as well as British, balance-of-payments data. Thus, it may be that recent British current account deficits are somewhat overstated, and this qualification to what follows should be borne in mind.

Trade balances are influenced by a number of factors which preclude any straightforward identification of an increasing trade deficit with a deterioration of productive performance. The manufacturing trade balance depends not only on developments in that sector but also on the position in non-manufacturing. Recent research has identified a strong tendency since the early post-war years for autonomous improvements in Britain's trading position in food and raw materials to reduce the manufacturing trade balance at an equilibrium exchange rate (Rowthorn and Wells, 1987). Such trends were reinforced by the implications of the discovery of North Sea oil and the OPEC oil price shock of the late 1970s (Bean, 1987).

Macro-economic Policy's Effects on the Balance of Payments

When considering the current account of the balance of payments, it is important to remember that it will be influenced by macro-economic management, including both exchange rate policy and the pace at which overall demand is allowed to expand, as well as by the balance of domestic savings and investments. These factors will, of course, have an impact on both manufacturing and non-manufacturing trade balances. Thus, paradoxically, a deficit could actually reflect improved growth potential which gives rise to expectations of higher future incomes and thus increased present consumption financed by borrowing. This would lower savings relative to investment and lead to inflows of capital from abroad. Financial de-regulation

[54]

and belief in the 'Thatcher Miracle' seem to have had a large effect of this kind in the mid-to-late 1980s (Muellbauer and Murphy, 1990). At the same time, excessive growth of domestic demand appears to have accounted for half or more of the balance-of-payments deficit (Barrell and Wren-Lewis, 1989).

Econometric investigations which focus on the export performance of manufacturing alone have in fact found evidence of substantial improvements in the 1980s. This can also be seen in the stabilisation of Britain's share of world trade shown in Table 7 (above, p. 20). For example, Britton and Anderton report that

'Re-estimation of the equation for manufactures of exports confirms that the tendency for British industry to lose market share at any constant level of relative prices came to an end in the 1980s' (1990, p. 4).

Moreover, the structure of British manufacturing trade also reflects some strengths overlooked by those who take a gloomy view. The export-import balance was most healthy in the late 1980s for those goods which the European Commission categorises as of 'strong' rather than 'moderate' or 'weak' demand growth (European Commission, 1990, Tables 12, 14, 16). Table 18 shows that relative British market shares (revealed comparative advantage) in high-technology industries, while less impressive than the Japanese or American, nonetheless look very respectable on a European basis. The strong showing in pharmaceuticals is particularly striking.

Independent estimates of the *'Fundamental Equilibrium Exchange Rate (FEER)'** made by Barrell and Wren-Lewis (1989) and by Church (1992) indicate that, after the de-industrialisation of the early Thatcher years and the oil price crash of the mid-1980s but prior to the overheating of the 'Lawson Boom' years, the economy was in a position where external payments balance and unemployment at the NAIRU could co-exist. In other words, it appeared as if the economy had been through a successful process of structural change while improving its productivity performance before ill-advised macro-economic policy generated a deterioration in the current account.

Changing export capabilities and/or import propensities as growth takes place at home and abroad may require adjustments to the terms of trade (that is, the real exchange rate). In the long run, as was noted in Section II, that is the appropriate adjustment in the face of the differing trade elasticities highlighted by

[Cont'd. on p. 58]

[55]

TABLE 18

REVEALED COMPARATIVE ADVANTAGE IN HIGH-TECHNOLOGY INDUSTRIES:
SELECTED COUNTRIES, 1979 AND 1988

SITC		UK		Germany		Japan		USA	
		1979	1988	1979	1988	1979	1988	1979	1988
515	Radioactive Materials	1	2	86	83	88	86	8	14
531	Synthetic Organic Dyestuffs	18	12	1	1	50	44	69	69
541	Medical/Pharmaceutical	14	6	44	44	71	64	20	15
581	Plastic Materials	48	45	10	24	46	49	37	24
711	Power Generators	7	18	37	48	38	26	5	5
714	Office Machines	15	22	63	75	29	8	2	3
715	Metalworking Machinery	51	56	4	9	23	7	33	30
722	Electric Power Machinery	38	46	19	37	25	12	21	21
724	Telecoms. Apparatus	59	74	62	74	5	2	32	24
729	Other Electrical Machinery	64	49	51	65	21	5	12	8
734	Aircraft	9	16	73	89	87	76	1	1
861	Scientific Instruments	23	19	30	35	26	14	6	6
864	Watches and Clocks	85	86	77	81	9	10	82	83
	Median	23	22	44	48	29	14	21	15

[56]

SITC		Italy 1979	Italy 1988	Sweden 1979	Sweden 1988	Switzerland 1979	Switzerland 1988
515	Radioactive Materials	89	89	60	59	80	83
531	Synthetic Organic Dyestuffs	79	83	86	85	2	2
541	Medical/Pharmaceutical	49	51	37	23	5	4
581	Plastic Materials	46	46	40	42	43	39
711	Power Generators	62	69	31	27	31	54
714	Office Machines	53	64	26	51	62	74
715	Metalworking Machinery	34	24	26	34	8	7
722	Electric Power Machinery	54	59	31	34	10	15
724	Telecoms. Apparatus	72	80	11	29	46	68
729	Other Electrical Machinery	66	66	60	64	31	44
734	Aircraft	79	84	86	68	76	77
861	Scientific Instruments	76	69	42	39	12	14
864	Watches and Clocks	83	87	86	85	1	1
	Median	66	69	40	42	31	39

Source: Derived from United Nations (1984) (1990); 1 = highest rank, 89 = lowest for each country. Hi-tech industries as designated by Eurostat (1989).

TABLE 19
TERMS-OF-TRADE ADJUSTMENTS TO
REAL GDP GROWTH
(per cent per year)

	1950-73	*1973-87*
France	0·0	–0·2
Germany	0·5	–0·1
Japan	0·4	–0·2
UK	**0·0**	**0·0**
USA	0·0	–0·2

Source: Derived from OECD (1970) (1991a); a rising price of exports relative to imports increases real income and increases growth of real income above that of real product (GDP) by an amount which depends on how big exports and imports are relative to home production. The estimates in the Table use the Hamada-Iwata method of dealing with the index number problems involved in this adjustment (see Irwin (1991)).

Thirlwall (1979). Changing terms of trade affect real purchasing power and mean that growth of real GDP has to be corrected before real income growth is measured. Table 19 reviews the impact of this correction on the growth of real income, taking into account both movements of the terms of trade and their significance in terms of the ratio of international trade to total activity. Evidently, allowing for this effect increases the gap between Britain's performance and that of Germany and Japan in the 'Golden Age' but in 1973-87 there was a small reversal of this position largely due to North Sea oil.

So, through to the mid-1980s, 20 years of de- industrialisation did not appear to have reduced the growth of real income through terms-of-trade effects. The implications for future real income growth are, however, rather less favourable and to that extent the worries about the manufacturing base emphasised by House of Lords (1985) may have some validity. Thus, Church (1992) estimates that since the early 1980s, even allowing for better exporting performance, the FEER has been falling at a trend rate of about 1·5 per cent per year and that this is likely to continue through the 1990s primarily because of a very strong propensity to import manufactures: the implication is a future terms-of-trade reduction to real GDP growth of about 0·4 per cent per year.

A Balance-of-Payments Constraint on Growth?

In Section II it was argued that balance-of-payments-constrained growth models were not helpful in understanding or explaining post-war experience, in particular because in the long run real wages are not rigid and the real exchange rate can adjust the balance of payments so that the growth of real GDP can realise its supply-side potential. However, this argument may not apply so readily to the UK in the 1990s.

Estimates of the FEER suggest the need for a steady depreciation over time if external and internal balance is to be maintained. Moreover, exchange rate policy since the late 1980s has created a position where the pound is well above its FEER. In common with many other writers, Church (1992, p. 66) found that entry to the ERM was at a level of 5-10 per cent overvaluation and the subsequent decline of the dollar has exacerbated this situation.

Inside the ERM en route to EMU we must have expected that achieving changes in the equilibrium real exchange rate against our partner countries could not be done by varying the nominal exchange rate but only through differences in the rate of inflation. Assuming that the inflation rate of ERM countries is set by the Bundesbank in the medium term at a level close to zero, this could well have implied the need for future British price and possibly even wage increases to be negative given the possible trend for the future FEER. In such circumstances the difficulties of adjustment feared by Thirlwall may indeed be serious; history suggests that reducing nominal wages is in general very difficult.

Empirical investigation of the last three decades suggests that shocks, especially on the supply side, to the British and German economies are only weakly correlated and that as a result the equilibrium real exchange rate between the two countries has varied considerably over time (Bayoumi and Eichengreen, 1992). Against this background, joining in a currency union with Germany would risk imposing unnecessary deflationary pressure on the British economy.

In sum, it appears likely that in the aftermath of de-industrialisation in the UK there will be a tendency towards adverse terms-of-trade effects in the 1990s. Membership of the ERM would make it more likely than in the past that these tendencies could, at least for a time, be converted into a Thirlwall-type balance-of-payments constraint on growth. Out-side the ERM there is even less reason than before, given weaker trade unions, to fear that real wage rigidity could give rise to this problem.

Learning Effects, Externalities and Future Technological Capabilities

Many authors have pointed to the long-term dangers of deflationary British government policy and the high exchange rate of the early 1980s in an environment where government support for industry was generally being withdrawn. It can be argued, in principle, that the 'cold bath' of the period had good short-term pay-offs in productivity increase but that they were at the expense of long-term growth. That is essentially the House of Lords (1985) view and is captured theoretically in the model of Krugman (1987) which forms the basis of Figure 1 in Section II (see Box 1 above, pp. 36-37).

There will be greater reason to worry about contractions of the manufacturing base arising from such shocks the more of the following conditions apply.

○ There are strong learning effects in productivity growth.

○ Productivity growth potential varies a great deal between sectors.

○ International trade leads to complete specialisation in production in different countries.

○ There are external economies in production.

○ Capital markets are short-termist.

If all these circumstances prevail, a strong case for government intervention can be made and the Thatcherite policies of the early 1980s would indeed have entailed serious risks of substantial permanent damage to growth prospects.

Research in the economics of technology certainly provides examples where such conditions have applied, perhaps the best recently documented being that of nuclear power reactors (Cowan, 1990). Here the combination of learning effects and American subsidies to light-water technology succeeded in capturing virtually the whole market for this technique even though it was probably not inherently superior to the British alternative.

More generally, it has been suggested that high-technology industries are characterised by strong dynamic learning effects

(Mowery and Rosenberg, 1989) and spillovers of R+D (Jaffe, 1986). The conventional wisdom is that industries in this group will be important in generating new industries and as catalysts to change in old industries (OECD, 1992). Increasingly also, the literature of the economics of technology emphasises the crucial rôle of established in-house expertise in taking advantage of new technological possibilities (Dosi, 1988). At the same time, research into the process of exit from British industry through bankruptcy has found evidence of an increasing tendency for short-run cash-flow considerations to dominate rather than the long-run viability of firms (Turner *et al.*, 1992).

Empirical Support for Krugman-Lucas – 'Special Cases'

There is thus some empirical support for a Krugman-Lucas view of the world. Before we accord it paradigmatic status, however, we should recognise that the cases cited are special rather than general ones. In general, the world does not conform closely to the five conditions laid out above, as both authors freely acknowledge in their papers.

Four points in particular should be recognised.

(i) Cross-section econometric investigation of productivity growth in British manufacturing over the period 1954-86 rejects the hypotheses of externalities to physical capital formation and increasing returns to scale and also reveals correlations of output and productivity growth inconsistent with strong and pervasive learning effects (Oulton, 1992).

(ii) Britain's position in international trade, in common with all major OECD economies, is by no means one of complete specialisation in particular categories. On the contrary, the striking feature of our manufactured trade is the high degree of intra-industry trade—that is, substantial exports and imports are found in most sectors (Greenaway and Milner, 1984).

(iii) A recent survey by a leading proponent of new growth theory describes empirical evidence of external benefits from *learning by doing** as still very scanty (Grossman, 1990, p. 109).

(iv) As Table 20 shows, although high-technology industry is a smaller proportion of British manufacturing than in Germany or Japan, it is not negligible and its share rose

TABLE 20

VALUE ADDED IN HIGH-TECHNOLOGY INDUSTRY,
1979 AND 1988

| | % of Manufacturing | | % of GDP | |
	1979	1988	1979	1988
Germany	16·5	20·3	5·6	6·3
Japan	16·6	22·9	4·9	6·6
UK	**15·0**	**19·7**	**3·7**	**3·9**
USA	20·8	24·4	4·8	4·7

Source: OECD (1992b) (1984); high-technology defined as in OECD (1992a).

during the 1980s—a point which goes with the picture of revealed comparative advantage given in Table 18.

More generally, it must be questioned whether the variation in productivity growth across sectors is large enough to make observed differences in structural change between countries a big factor in future growth prospects. High-technology sectors in Britain in 1980-89 had a labour productivity growth rate about 1·3 per cent per year higher than the median for all manufacturing (calculated from Davis *et al.*, 1992, Table 5)—that is, an increase in their relative weight to Japanese proportions would have had only a tiny impact on aggregate growth.

Table 8 (above, p. 21) demonstrated that the UK had experienced higher-than-average de-industrialisation since 1973. Using the same sources as for Table 4, an arithmetic calculation of the effect on productivity growth of supposing that the UK had de-industrialised at the average rate and that the gap between sectoral productivity growth rates had stayed the same shows that the impact would have been to raise the UK's overall growth rate by only 0·15 per cent per year. That is likely to have been an overestimate of the true impact, both because of undermeasurement of service sector productivity growth and because no allowance is made for diminishing marginal productivity of labour within sectors.

The future implications of de-industrialisation for productivity growth are uncertain. Lagging service sector productivity growth during the 1980s may have been a reflection partly of once-and-for-all catch-up in manufacturing under the impact of the

Thatcher shock. On the other hand, there is still a much greater productivity gap with America in manufacturing than in services (Tables 5 and 6, above, pp. 18-19), so that there may still be considerable unexhausted catch-up potential and thus prospective productivity growth in manufacturing. As remarked in Section II, a lot depends on whether the convergence process will ultimately see an erosion of the American lead.

Conclusions

This section has suggested that de-industrialisation in the UK may have some adverse long-run implications. The smaller manufacturing base will probably mean losses to real income growth from terms-of-trade effects in the 1990s. In combination with inappropriate macro-economic policies, there is some risk of a period in which a balance-of-payments constraint on growth may operate. There is a possibility of a Krugman-Lucas effect operating to slow down future growth although, on the evidence of past experience, this is likely to be small. Taking a long-run view does then suggest a slightly less favourable view of the 1980s contribution to British economic growth than Section III presented. Even so, it does not seem to justify the apocalyptic 'House of Lords View'. Does it imply the necessity for a return to high-profile industrial policy?

V. DO WE NEED A NEW INDUSTRIAL POLICY?

Market Distortions, Macro-Policy and the 'House of Lords View'

Proponents of the 'House of Lords View' across all political parties typically argue that changes in government policy are desirable to address the apparent decline in the UK's manufacturing base. Indeed, the House of Lords Select Committee on Science and Technology concluded that

'The present lack of Government commitment, support and assistance to industry are damaging to our national interest' (1991, p. 43).

Clearly, many types of government activity impinge on industrial costs, perhaps as an unintended side-effect of the pursuit of disparate goals. These costs may be particularly onerous to small businesses. Quite possibly British industry is vulnerable to price distortions arising from the pursuit of market power by nationalised industries or inadequately regulated sectors. In assessing costs and benefits of policy decisions, too little weight may in the past have been placed on these industrial implications. For example, while the promise of privatisation may have been good for productivity growth, as was argued in Section III, seen from the perspective of avoiding distortions in markets it was much less satisfactory, notably in the energy sector (Vickers and Yarrow, 1988). Similarly, it is important that government does not inadvertently handicap British industrialists through poor macro-economic policy based, perhaps, on inaccurate Treasury forecasts.

If the notion of greater government support for industry is construed as eliminating policy errors of these kinds, then it would certainly be welcome. It is clear, however, that the House of Lords view goes considerably further than this and veers off down the path of interventionism and protectionism. My purpose in this section is to assess the case for a renewal of the latter type of industrial policy.

Government Policy 'Idiosyncratic'

The Labour Party firmly supports such a change in direction and sees recent government policy as idiosyncratic:

> 'Only the Conservatives remain outside this new consensus, still opposed to any industrial policy. Our first move in government will therefore be to bring together industry and finance into a manufacturing partnership, building on the consensus which already exists' (1992, pp. 12-13).

It goes on to promise, amongst other things, new tax incentives for investment in manufacturing, tax credits for additional expenditures on R+D, and the establishment of regional development agencies in England. Mr Michael Heseltine, the President of the Board of Trade, while out of office, also seemed to advocate a return to significantly greater intervention than would have found favour with his predecessor:

> 'There are industries, such as the steel industry, the car industry and the airframe industry, which cannot be allowed to fail if Britain is to remain an advanced economy' (1987, p. 111).

In Section IV it was argued that fears about the growth effects of de-industrialisation are generally much exaggerated. Nevertheless, it is possible that allowing too large a rôle to market forces in determining industrial structure will have adverse implications for future growth, giving *prima facie* grounds for a return to industrial policy. This section considers the arguments in more detail by probing further into the intellectual case for intervention, reviewing the past experience and evaluating some policy options. In so doing it will be as well to bear in mind the possibility that the proposed cures may be worse than the disease.

Market Failure as a Justification for Industrial Policy

In an economy characterised by a *Pareto-optimal allocation of resources** the division of output between manufacturing and services would reflect consumers' preferences and real resource costs and for each item the marginal benefit of consumption would equal the marginal cost of production. In such a situation, there would be no reason to regard a switch of output away from services into manufacturing as welfare-improving. The classic resource allocation ground for intervention is to rectify a case of market failure where these efficiency conditions are not met. It is

[65]

Rent-Snatching through Subsidies

In Figure 2(i), if Boeing is already established in the industry, there is no incentive for Airbus to enter without subsidies because, if it does, it will make inadequate returns (−5). A commitment by European governments to pay the subsidy changes the pay-offs. Airbus is now better off producing than not producing whatever Boeing does and will definitely enter. Boeing is thus certain to lose money if it does produce and will therefore exit if it has no access to subsidy. Rents (i.e., profits in

Figure 2:
Subsidised Entry into the Civil Airliner Market

(i) *Successful Intervention*

	Airbus	
	Produce	Don't Produce
Boeing Produce	(−5, −5)	(100, 0)
Boeing Don't Produce	(0, 100)	(0, 0)

(a) No Subsidies

	Airbus	
	Produce	Don't Produce
Boeing Produce	(−5, 20)	(100, 0)
Boeing Don't Produce	(0, 125)	(0, 0)

(b) With Subsidies to Airbus

therefore important that advocates of industrial policy should identify clearly which are the market failures they wish to remedy and demonstrate that the selected policy instruments are appropriately targeted.

A well-known idea is that 'infant industries', whose costs will fall with experience, should be temporarily protected if in this way they can ultimately establish a comparative advantage. This suggestion might be justified in a Krugman/Lucas model. However, learning effects do not of and by themselves clinch the case for this kind of intervention; if the gains are appropriable by the firm doing the learning, then well-functioning capital markets will finance worthwhile infant industries. A case for intervention would have to be based either on external spillovers excess of those required to stay in business in the long run) for Airbus of 125 are acquired for a subsidy of only 25.

If pay-offs are as in Figure 2(ii), however, the same subsidy produces a different outcome. In this case it is insufficient to drive Boeing out because Boeing still makes excess profits (5) even if Airbus enters and both produce. Here the rents of only 5 for Airbus are less than the subsidy. In other words, governments may have the potential to influence entry and exit decisions in oligopolistic industries. Nonetheless, such interventions will not always pay off and, if their size or timing is inappropriate, may be expensive failures (see below, p. 70).

Figure 2 (continued):

(ii) *Unsuccessful Intervention*

	Airbus				Airbus	
	Produce	Don't Produce			Produce	Don't Produce
Produce (5, −20)	(125, 0)			Produce (5, 5)	(125, 0)	
Boeing				Boeing		
Don't Produce (0, 100)	(0, 0)			Don't Produce (0, 125)	(0, 0)	
	(a) No Subsidies				*(b) With Subsidies to Airbus*	

Source: Krugman and Obstfeld (1991, pp. 270-72).
Note: Pay-offs in terms of super-normal profits are listed with Boeing first in each case and in both examples for the 'with subsidies' case a government subsidy of 25 is paid to Airbus but nothing to Boeing.

of knowledge such that social returns were larger than private returns or on seeking to compensate for capital market imperfections. Similar arguments apply to proposals to subsidise research and development in high-technology industries.

A more recent argument for an industrial policy is based on the analysis of strategic behaviour under oligopoly, a market structure which is quite common in high-technology industries. The basic point can be illustrated with an example popularised by Krugman and reproduced in Figure 2 (see Box 2).

Even where there appears to be a straightforward case for intervention to correct divergences of social and private returns or to capture rents from abroad, there are typically risks of welfare losses, especially given the likely presence of imperfect

[67]

and indeed asymmetric information. In particular, as noted in Section III, there are dangers that, if discretionary subsidies are available, firms will devote insufficient effort to cost-reduction and that low-effort bargaining equilibria are sustained while at the same time lobbying activities are encouraged. Attempts to improve allocative efficiency may sometimes promote Eurosclerosis.

These considerations strengthen the case for agreed international free trade rules or at least for explicit international regulation of any departures from free trade. Pre-commitment by government to such arrangements can take away the potential for this tendency to the creation and dissipation of rents. In principle, this may be a gain from the European Single Market Programme and probably has been one of the favourable effects of the Treaty of Rome (Adams, 1989).

Past Experience of Industrial Policy

In Section III it was suggested that the record of British industrial policy in the pre-1979 period was deeply unimpressive in terms of its impact in raising the growth rate. It should be remembered that its justification was generally in terms of arguments similar to the 'House of Lords View' and that industrial policies are inherently protectionist. Policy initiatives were intended to enhance the manufacturing base by combatting capital market imperfections and influencing strategic entry/exit decisions in key industries, thus shifting resources into sectors with substantial learning effects and technological spillovers.

Two sectors given much support in post-war Britain were the aerospace industry and nuclear power. In both, economists have been highly sceptical of the benefits of the expenditure. Hayward (1983) catalogues the disappointing outcomes of support for civil aircraft, highlighted, of course, by the disastrous Concorde project. Stoneman observes that

'the largest UK civil R+D programme we have had has been the AGR programme for nuclear reactors, which has produced nothing of any commercial value whatever over 20 years' (1991, p. 16).

Because of the special status of defence, government has tended to accept industrial policy arguments put forward by domestic contractors which have encouraged rent-seeking. Smith (1990, p. 195) points out that many of these projects were notorious for cost overruns and performance failures, culminating in the

Nimrod débâcle. Indeed, the evidence in general is of very little in the way of positive externalities from the government's large defence-related R+D programme (ACOST, 1989).

British attempts to provide support for British technology have frequently failed to achieve successful entry into industries dominated on a world scale by the USA. For example, American subsidies, linked in part to defence requirements, overwhelmed the British nuclear programme (Cowan, 1990), and the advantage of the large domestic American defence market for computers rendered our subsidies relatively ineffective in that industry (Hendry, 1989).

Nor is there much comfort to be obtained by reflecting on the record of Britain's state investment companies, the Industrial Reorganisation Commission (1966-71) and the National Enterprise Board (1975-81). Hindley and Richardson (1983) showed how relatively low the returns were on government-backed mergers in which soft loans were involved, while Morris and Stout (1985, p. 873) concluded that 'through these institutions it was losers like Rolls-Royce, British Leyland and Alfred Herbert who picked Ministers'. Similarly, as Vickers and Yarrow (1988) observe, it is quite implausible that the hugely inferior profit performance of nationalised industries relative to private sector companies can be justified by social returns to their investment.

Failure of Industrial Policy: European Examples

Appraisals of industrial policy in other European countries have also produced damning reports. Geroski and Jacquemin see the promotion of national champions leaving Europe 'with a population of sleepy industrial giants who were ill-equipped to meet the challenge of the 1970s and 1980s' (1989, p. 303), and in activities like semi-conductors being quite ineffective as a means of gaining market share from Japan or the USA. Hindley concludes that

> 'state investment companies have not improved the operation of the capital market but rather have caused misallocation of capital' (1983, p. 24).

German policies to subsidise high technology sectors like aircraft, nuclear energy and telecommunications have been no more successful than the British ones (Horn, 1987).

The preliminary conclusions of research on international

[69]

trade policy in the presence of imperfect competition should also be given due weight. While the prevalence of oligopoly and intra-industry trade appears to make economic theory ambivalent about the benefits of free trade (Figure 2), in practice the evidence is that the case is strengthened. Richardson, after surveying the recent literature, concluded:

> 'The easy presumption of gains in a perfectly competitive environment vanishes under imperfect competition. Yet . . . empirical research has generated a replacement presumption: as a rule, trade liberalization still leads to gains, which may be two to three times larger than those estimated under perfect competition' (1989, p. 8).

In particular, these larger gains are achieved through the effects of free entry and exit leading to rationalisation of industrial structure. These effects probably played an important part in the OECD countries' exceptionally rapid catch-up growth in the 1950s and 1960s (Crafts, 1992). Such a process is central in the European Commission's report on the impact of 1992 (Emerson, 1988). Yet it is antithetical to the traditional conception of industrial policy as practised by European countries.

Capturing rents is also not as easy as sometimes thought. The famous Boeing/Airbus example of Figure 2 (see Box 2) has been subjected to empirical analysis: it is unclear that Airbus subsidies have as yet actually produced welfare gains for Europe (Pomfret, 1991). A European presence in the civil airliner market remains, but on the other hand Boeing has not been forced out.

On balance, then, experience suggests that it is sensible to retain a presumption in favour of free trade policies and to be sceptical of the claims of those advocating active industrial policies. In particular, not only is Silberston (1981) right to emphasise that UK industrial policy mostly propped up declining industries but also the UK's selective support policies for high-technology industry have generally delivered most disappointing results.

Current Industrial Policies

Today industrial policy affecting UK manufacturing is carried out both by the British government and by the European Community. As far as domestic policy is concerned, there was both a large reduction in spending on industrial policy and a substantial re-orientation of that policy during the 1980s; these

TABLE 21

DEPARTMENT OF TRADE AND INDUSTRY EXPENDITURE

(£ million, 1988-89 prices)

	1981/2	1986/7	1990/1
1. Regional and General Industrial Support	1,002·8	477·0	294·5
2. Support for Aerospace, Shipbuilding, Steel, Vehicles	1,253·5	952·9	136·7
3. Support for Industry (including Innovation, Space)	285·7	346·5	271·6
4. Other	165·1	276·7	347·3
	2,707·1	2,053·1	1,050·1

Source: House of Lords (1991).

changes are reflected in Table 21 and are well described in Shepherd (1987) and House of Lords (1991).

The general thrust of the changes was to reduce support for investment in physical capital relative to R+D and human capital and to cut regional policy and other aid to declining industries—hence the big reduction in spending in categories 1 and 2 of Table 21. Support for innovation is mainly in category 3. Here moves were made to change direction towards facilitating the diffusion of knowledge rather than to subsidise commercial development. The new emphasis on technology transfer rather than prestige projects is in line with the recommendations of critics of earlier policies such as Ergas (1987).

In general, this reshaping of industrial policy appears likely to have targeted subsidy more closely on reducing market failures arising from externalities. Ceasing massively to subsidise physical capital but continuing to support other forms of investment is in line with the findings of the new growth economics summarised in Section II. Eliminating support for 'lame ducks' can, in the context of the UK's earlier history, be expected to have had beneficial effects on strengthening efforts to reduce costs and overmanning; here British Steel is the exemplar. Sensibly, government gave up trying to pick winners.

Changing this policy mix in ways recently advocated, for example by the Labour Party, seems of doubtful value. Consider a proposal to give temporary 100 per cent first year allowances for plant and machinery in manufacturing. Young estimates that this would raise investment in the first year by 6·8 per cent, partly brought forward from Year 2. As he points out:

> 'changes to the corporate tax system have a relatively small effect on the user cost of capital which in turn has a relatively small effect on investment' (1992, p. 22).

Given the weakness of the general evidence for externalities to physical investment (Oulton, 1992) and worries about cushioning inefficient management (Hitchens *et al.*, 1990), this is an unattractive proposal whether thought of as a supply-side measure or a Keynesian stimulus. Similarly, Stoneman (1991, p. 18), who is rightly keen to emphasise the likelihood of market failures relating to technological advance, nevertheless agrees with the Inland Revenue that generalised tax credits are not an efficient way to stimulate R+D.

EC Moves to Encourage Collaboration in High-Tech Industries

In the 1980s there were also important developments at the EC level. In particular, there were significant moves to support internationally collaborative R+D in high-technology industries through programmes such as ESPRIT in microelectronics, EUREKA in biotechnology, HDTV, robotics, etc., and JESSI in semiconductors. At least in terms of attempts to capture rents (or avoid paying them to the USA or Japan), such policies may have a justification and may be more likely to succeed at a European than a British level. Thus, the survival of Airbus suggests, for example, that a European programme of support for a rival nuclear technology might have succeeded in the 1950s and offset the subsidies to and strong learning effects in the American technology (Cowan, 1990). Similarly, Flamm (1990) sees hope of success for European industrial policy initiatives in semiconductors.

The incipient tendency to transfer industrial policy to the EC level will be reinforced by the Single Market Programme which will restrict industrial policy interventions at the national level by reducing the scope for protectionism, notably by opening up public procurement to competition and by tighter control of state aids. Indeed, in general the EC could operate increasingly to limit the rent-seeking power of industrial lobbies on the UK government by tieing ministerial hands.

Unfortunately, the Europeanisation of industrial policies carries with it serious problems. The EC is organised in a bureaucratic mode which has encouraged the formation of rent-seeking interest groups and cannot provide the same centralised procurement policies that Federal defence expenditure in the USA has used to support new technologies (Peirce, 1991). Moreover, moves towards ever-closer integration are likely to bring with them increased pressures from and funding for disadvantaged regions which may soften firms' budget constraints (Rodrik, 1990, p. 360). The substantial discretion enjoyed by the European Commission is also conducive to rent-seeking, as is highlighted by, for example, the conduct of EC anti-dumping cases (Eymann and Schuknecht, 1990).

A régime for the conduct of a more satisfactory European industrial policy with less protection for the inefficient producer could (but probably will not) be created by appropriate reforms. These would include further strengthening of the GATT and European competition policy, much stricter limitations on discretionary action by the Commission and increased transparency of decision-making, and public involvement of the competition directorate in evaluating the costs of industrial policy (Montagnon, 1990).

Conclusions

A recent critical review of past UK industrial policy concluded that

> 'it would be wrong to infer from the generally unconvincing track record of industrial policies that it is an approach which is inherently flawed' (Begg, 1992, p. 45).

If this were the case, then the arguments for a return to a more interventionist stance would be more persuasive. Unfortunately, although some of the failings of UK industrial policies should be blamed on inexperience or bad luck, it seems likely that there are inherent difficulties with such policies.

Vickers and Yarrow's excellent (1988) analysis of the principal-agent issue under imperfect information in the control of nationalised industries reveals the problems which beset industrial policy generally. Politicians' incentives to win votes encourage excessive subsidisation of producer interests and cannot be effectively monitored or deterred by the mass of voters on whom the costs fall. *The availability of subsidies makes budget constraints softer and is likely to lead both to too much investment and to bargaining equilibria with lower levels of effort.*

The implication is that the costs of industrial policy are generally likely to be large. Indeed, they may exceed the benefits: in earlier sections we saw that the arguments that there had been a catastrophic erosion of the manufacturing base and that externalities are large and pervasive in manufacturing were much exaggerated. If there is to be interventionist industrial policy, it is important that the intervention is targeted on specific market failures, tightly cash-limited and subject to independent public scrutiny and audit. Accepting EC restraints on Britain's use of such policies is desirable, as are serious efforts to reform the EC's own industrial policy process.

Where Begg (1992) is on firmer ground is in his insistence that policy should consider the wide array of influence on factor accumulation. It seems obvious that industrial policy as conventionally envisaged—for example, subsidies to manufacturing investment generally, selective intervention to aid particular firms or types of R+D, aids for the diffusion of knowledge, and so on—does not address some of the most important determinants of willingness to make long-term investments which, as Section III reported, continued to be a striking weakness of the UK through the 1980s. These factors are essentially to do with institutional structures which encourage *short-termism**.

Short-Termism

Two institutional features which encourage short-termism in investment have had much attention recently. One is the unique exposure of quoted British companies to hostile takeover. Mayer (1992), in a careful review of the evidence, concludes that large firms, which are important in high-technology industries, feel compelled to maintain dividends and forgo investment opportunities in R+D and training, unlike other European firms. The second, emphasised by Soskice (1989) as playing an important part in the persistence of a low level of skills, is the relative absence of long-term consensual relationships between British firms and their workers, leading to high levels of job turnover and poaching of trained employees. And it is reflected in the much smaller wage gaps between skilled adult workers and unskilled young workers in Britain than in Germany (Wagner,

1991). Addressing policy reforms to these issues is likely to be more productive than going back to traditional modes of industrial policy.

Rapid future growth in Britain will have to be based on total factor productivity growth and on continuing the more rapid catch-up of leading countries which started in the 1980s. This will be helped by policies which facilitate rapid technology transfer and impeded by policies which encourage rent-seeking and restrictive practices. Judged on these criteria, from 1945 to 1979 the UK's supply-side policies and institutional structures served us badly. On balance, the reforms of the 1980s, including the reshaping of industrial policy, improved matters. The main thrust of future strategy to promote growth should not be more subsidy for manufacturing or high technology but rather the pursuit of multilateral international agreements to reduce the extent of government support for industry and to promote freer trade.

VI. CONCLUSIONS

The UK economy has been through a traumatic recession. Not surprisingly, that experience has led to considerable scepticism about both economic policy and the achievements of the 1980s. Commentators now tend to emphasise the contraction in the relative size of the industrial sector and the increased trade deficit rather more and the revival of manufacturing productivity much less than they did a few years ago. As always in hard times, there are renewed calls for government interventionism and protectionism to save jobs. Changing fashions among economic theorists, prompted by economic decline in the United States relative to Japan, have produced new models of trade and growth which give better intellectual reasons for doubting the virtues of free trade and market forces in delivering fast growth.

Nevertheless, this study argues that the present grief stems largely from macro-economic mistakes in exchange rate/interest rate policies which first require to be corrected rather than being compounded by distortions introduced into micro-economic policy. It is important not to forget the lessons of the pre-1979 period, whilst also accepting that there can be market failures and that government has a positive part to play in enhancing future growth prospects.

The implications of de-industrialisation for future growth prospects are rarely examined carefully enough by those who fear the consequences; certainly this is true of the influential House of Lords reports reviewed here. The main channels through which adverse effects might operate are declining terms of trade, missing out on infant industries with high future productivity growth, and failure to benefit from spillovers which raise returns to investment. While the old-fashioned balance-of-payments-constrained growth hypotheses appear too pessimistic about the adjustment capabilities of the economy, new models associated in particular with Krugman and Lucas raise new worries that 1980s policy may have veered too far in the direction of the *laissez-faire*.

The Thatcher Experiment of the 1980s significantly enhanced productivity growth. Better performance came from an intensification of competitive pressures on management, a weakening of trade union bargaining power and a retreat from the unsuccessful interventionist policies of the 1960s and 1970s. There was a substantial shake-out of inefficiencies which had previously been allowed to persist. It is important not to return to the *status quo ante* 1979.

The UK has a high propensity to import manufactured goods which seems to require the real exchange rate to decline over time. The resulting loss of purchasing power over imports will reduce the rate of future real income growth, perhaps by as much as 0·4 per cent per year. Nevertheless, this does not of itself create a case for government intervention. This should be confined to remedying identifiable market failures, for example where social and private returns to investment diverge. Moreover, if intervening it is important not to reduce the pressure on firms to seek further cost reductions. Nationalisation, picking winners and protecting lame ducks in the 1970s were highly inefficient policies. By contrast, the rehabilitation of British Steel in the 1980s, which might not have been achieved by the private market, was successful.

It remains to be seen quite how powerful is the empirical support for the new Krugman-Lucas arguments to justify infant industry policies. At present, the evidence is thin and hard to quantify. Given the endemic dangers of bureaucratically run industrial policies and the general desirability of working towards the strengthening of international arrangements to achieve multilateral disarmament in industrial subsidies, there is at best limited scope for active policy in this area.

Infant industry policies have most justification where capital markets are imperfect. International comparisons suggest the UK is relatively weak in long-term investments, including human capital and R+D, the factors emphasised by new growth theory as engines of long-term success and which have positive externalities (Van de Klundert and Smulders, 1992; O'Mahony, 1992a). Policy efforts should increasingly be directed towards reforming institutional structures to reduce short-termism and to strengthen human capital formation whilst retaining the disciplines of competition.

GLOSSARY

Atkinson Index of Inequality: This is based on judgements as to how much total income society is prepared to lose in order to carry out a given re-distribution of income; detailed discussion of the formulae involved is in Beckerman (1980).

Cross-Sectional Study: A comparison based on examining performance of different sectors in the same time-period.

Dynamic Economies of Scale: The proposition that productivity increases as a result of a faster rate of growth of output.

Endogenous Growth Models: Models in which faster rates of accumulation of human and/or physical capital lead to persistently higher growth of output rather than being offset by diminishing returns.

Externalities: Costs or benefits affecting people other than the decision-maker him/herself. In the context of growth models the standard hypothesis is that those carrying out investment do not receive all the benefits which accrue to society as a whole.

Fundamental Equilibrium Exchange Rate (FEER): The concept of the Fundamental Equilibrium Exchange Rate seeks to measure the exchange rate which would permit a long-run sustainable balance-of-payments position to co-exist with the fullest utilisation rate of domestic resources consistent with stable inflation. It is estimated with regard both to the current account and the capital account.

Golden Age: This term is used to indicate a period when economic performance was unusually good throughout the OECD. In the context of this *Hobart Paper* the reference is to growth but, more generally, it might be noted that the early post-war years also saw good inflation and unemployment figures.

Heuristic Model: A suggestive scheme of explanation relying on intuition rather than a formalised, rigorous treatment.

Income Elasticity: The proportionate change in quantity

demanded relative to the proportionate change in income holding prices constant.

Keynesian Demand Shocks: Changes in the overall level of activity in the economy resulting from spending decisions by government and/or the private sector rather than changes in the economy's ability to produce.

Learning by Doing: Improvements in productivity based on the accumulation of experience in production with a given level of investment and technology.

New Growth Economics: The recent body of literature concerned with endogenous growth (*q.v.*).

Non-Accelerating Inflation Rate of Unemployment (NAIRU): The balance point of the labour market at which level of unemployment wage claims are consistent with a stable rate of inflation and the inflationary expectations of both firms and workers are realised.

Okun's Law: This states that in recessions output falls by more than employment while in booms output rises by more than employment.

Pareto-Optimal Allocation of Resources: A Pareto-Optimal allocation is one where it is impossible to make any one person better off except by making at least one other person worse off. The first-order conditions for this require that relative prices reflect both marginal rates of substitution of consumers and marginal rates of transformation in production.

Petro-Currency: A currency of an oil-producing country where the exchange rate tends to rise noticeably when the price of oil goes up.

Production-Function-Based Analysis: An investigation based on explicit assumptions concerning the mathematical nature of the relationship between the use of factors of production and output.

Short-Termism: A tendency to value returns to investment expected in the near future much more highly than returns in the distant future.

Technology Transfer: The successful application of methods of production initially discovered and implemented in another country.

Time-Series: Data on the behaviour of economic variables gathered in the form of observations in successive time-periods.

Total Factor Productivity (TFP): Output per unit of total input.

Verdoorn's Law: The hypothesis that growth of output per worker in industry increases as a result of faster industrial employment growth.

List of acronyms:

ESPRIT: European Strategic Programme in Information Technologies

EUREKA: European Research Co-operation Agency

HDTV: High Definition Television

JESSI: Joint European Submicron Silicon Initiative

QUESTIONS FOR DISCUSSION

1. Should we trust the market to decide the division of economic activity as between manufacturing and services?

2. Does the idea of protecting 'infant industries' justify establishing industrial policies?

3. Was slow growth in post-war Britain mainly due to inadequate levels of investment?

4. Did the Thatcher years produce an economy with permanently enhanced growth prospects?

5. What were the main failings in the industrial policies adopted by British governments prior to 1979?

6. Explain the Krugman-Lucas model of specialisation and growth. How useful is it in explaining why growth rates differ?

7. What is the 'House of Lords View' of the relationship between the manufacturing base and the rate of economic growth?

8. Why is the case for free trade less persuasive theoretically if industry is monopolistic?

9. In what main ways does the prevalence of 'asymmetric information' affect the design of industrial policy?

10. 'The recent recession has resulted from macro-economic policy errors. It does not imply the need for fundamental micro-economic policy changes.' Discuss.

REFERENCES/FURTHER READING

Abramovitz, M. (1986): 'Catching Up, Forging Ahead, and Falling Behind', *Journal of Economic History*, Vol. 46, pp. 385-406.

Adams, W.J. (1989): *Restructuring the French Economy*, Washington: Brookings Institution.

ACOST: Advisory Council on Science and Technology (1989): *Defence R & D: A National Resource*, London: HMSO.

Bacon, R. W. and Eltis, W. A. (1976): *Britain's Economic Problem: Too Few Producers*, London: Macmillan.

Baldwin, R. E. (1989): 'The Growth Effects of 1992', *Economic Policy*, Vol. 9, pp. 248-81.

Barnett, C. (1986): *The Audit of War*, London: Macmillan.

Barrell, R. and Wren-Lewis, S. (1989): 'Fundamental Equilibrium Exchange Rates for the G7', CEPR Discussion Paper No. 323.

Barro, R. and Sala-i-Martin, X. (1991): 'Convergence Across States and Regions', *Brookings Papers on Economic Activity*, Vol. 1, pp. 107-58.

Bayoumi, T. and Eichengreen, B. (1992): 'Shocking Aspects of European Monetary Unification', CEPR Discussion Paper No. 643.

Bean, C. (1987): 'The Impact of North Sea Oil', in R. Dornbusch and R. Layard (eds.), *The Performance of the British Economy*, Oxford: Clarendon Press.

Bean, C. and Symons, J. (1989): 'Ten Years of Mrs T.', CEPR Discussion Paper No. 316.

Beckerman, W. (1980): 'Comparative Growth Rates of "Measurable Economic Welfare": Some Experimental Calculations', in R. C. O. Matthews (ed.), *Economic Growth and Resources*, Vol. 2, London: Macmillan.

Begg, I. (1992): 'Industrial Investment and Supply-Side Policies in Europe', in A. Britton (ed.), *Industrial Investment as a Policy Objective*, London: NIESR.

Bishop, M. and Kay, J. (1988): *Does Privatization Work?*, London: London Business School.

Britton, A. and Anderton, R. (1990): 'The Balance of Payments and Economic Policy in Britain', NIESR Discussion Paper No. 187.

Broadberry, S. N. (1992a): 'Comparative Productivity Performance in Manufacturing since the Early Nineteenth Century: Europe and the United States', Warwick: University of Warwick (mimeo).

Broadberry, S. N. (1992b): 'Manufacturing and the Convergence Hypothesis: What the Long Run Data Show', Warwick Economic Research Paper, No. 393.

Brown, C. J. and Sheriff, T. D. (1979): 'De-Industrialisation: A Background Paper', in F. T. Blackaby (ed.), *De-Industrialisation*, London: Heinemann, pp. 233-62.

Brown, W. and Wadhwani, S. (1990): 'The Economic Effects of Industrial Relations Legislation Since 1979', *National Institute Economic Review*, No. 131, pp. 57-69.

Burton, John (1983): *Picking Losers . . .?*, Hobart Paper No. 99, London: Institute of Economic Affairs.

Central Statistical Office (1991): *Monthly Review of External Trade Statistics*, London.

Chandler, A. D. (1990): *Scale and Scope: The Dynamics of Industrial Capitalism*, Cambridge, MA.: Harvard University Press.

Chatterji, M. and Wickens, M. (1982): 'Productivity, Factor Transfers and Economic Growth in the UK', *Economica*, Vol. 49, pp. 21-38.

Chatterji, M. and Wickens, M. (1983): 'Verdoorn's Law and Kaldor's Law: A Revisionist Interpretation', *Journal of Post-Keynesian Economics*, Vol. 5, pp. 397-413.

Church, K. (1992): 'Properties of the Fundamental Equilibrium Exchange Rate in Models of the UK Economy', *National Institute Economic Review*, No. 141, pp. 62-70.

Confederation of British Industry (1977): *Britain Means Business*, London: CBI.

Cowan, R. (1990): 'Nuclear Power Reactors: A Study in Technological Lock-In', *Journal of Economic History*, Vol. 50, pp. 541-67.

Cowling, K., Stoneman, P., Cubbin, J., Cable, J., Hall, G., Domberger, S. and Dutton, P. (1980): *Mergers and Economic Performance*, Cambridge: Cambridge University Press.

Crafts, N. F. R. (1991): 'Economic Growth', in N. F. R. Crafts and N. W. C. Woodward (eds.), *The British Economy Since 1945*, Oxford: Clarendon Press.

Crafts, N. F. R. (1992): 'Productivity Growth Reconsidered', *Economic Policy*, Vol. 15, pp. 388-426.

Crafts, N. F. R. (1993): 'Was the Thatcher Experiment Worth It? British Economic Growth in a European Context', in D. Pilat, E. Szirmai and B. Van Ark (eds.), *Explaining Economic Growth*, Amsterdam: Elsevier.

Crafts, N. F. R. and Woodward, N. W. C. (1991): 'The British Economy Since 1945: Introduction and Overview', in N. F. R. Crafts and N. W. C. Woodward (eds.), *The British Economy Since 1945*, Oxford: Clarendon Press.

Davis, E., Flanders, S. and Star, J. (1992): 'British Industry in the 1980s', *Business Strategy Review*, Vol. 3, pp. 45-69.

De Long, J. B. and Summers, L. H. (1991): 'Equipment Investment and Economic Growth', *Quarterly Journal of Economics*, Vol. 106, pp. 445-502.

Dosi, G. (1988): 'Sources, Procedures and Microeconomic Effects of Innovation', *Journal of Economic Literature*, Vol. 26, pp. 1,120-1,171.

Dowrick, S. and Nguyen, D-T (1989): 'OECD Comparative Economic Growth 1950-85: Catch-Up and Convergence', *American Economic Review*, Vol. 79, pp. 1,010-1,030.

Durlauf, S. N. and Johnson, P. A. (1992): 'Local Versus Global Convergence Across National Economies', NBER Working Paper, No. 3996.

Emerson, M. (1988): *The Economics of 1992*, Oxford: Oxford University Press.

Englander, A. and Mittelstadt, A. (1988): 'Total Factor Productivity: Macroeconomic and Structural Aspects of the Slowdown', *OECD Economic Studies*, Vol. 10, pp. 7-56.

Ergas, H. (1987): 'Does Technology Policy Matter?', in B. R. Guile and H. Brooks (eds.), *Technology and Global Industry*, Washington: National Academy Press.

European Commission (1990): *Social Europe*, Luxembourg: EC.

Eurostat (1989): *Statistical Analysis of Extra-European 12 Trade in Hi-Tech Products*, Luxembourg.

Eymann, A. and Schuknecht, L. (1990): 'Antidumping Policy in the European Community: Political Discretion or Technical Determination', Universitat Konstanz Discussion Paper No. 106.

Flamm, K. (1990): 'Semiconductors', in G. C. Hufbauer (ed.), *Europe 1992: An American Perspective*, Washington: Brookings Institution.

Flanagan, R. J., Soskice, D. W. and Ulman, L. (1983): *Unionism, Economic Stabilization and Incomes Policies: The European Experience*, Washington: Brookings Institution.

Franks, J. and Mayer, C. (1990): 'Capital Markets and Corporate Control: A Study of France, Germany and the UK', *Economic Policy*, Vol. 10, pp. 191-231.

Geroski, P. and Jacquemin, A. P. (1989): 'Industrial Change, Barriers to Mobility and European Industrial Policy', in A. P. Jacquemin and A. Sapir (eds.), *The European Internal Market*, Oxford: Oxford University Press.

Greenhalgh, C. and Mavrotas, G. (1991): 'Workforce Training in the Thatcher Era—Market Forces and Market Failures', paper presented to the International Conference on the Economics of Training, Cardiff.

Greenaway, D. and Milner, C. R. (1984): 'A Cross-Section Study of Intra-Industry Trade in the UK', *European Economic Review*, Vol. 25, pp. 319-44.

Gregg, P., Machin, S. and Metcalf, D. (1991): 'Signals and Cycles: Productivity Growth and Changes in Union Status in British Companies, 1984-1989', University College London Discussion Paper No. 91-15.

Gribbin, J. D. (1978): 'The Postwar Revival of Competition Policy', *Government Economic Service Working Paper No. 19*.

Grossman, G. M. (1990): 'Promoting New Industrial Activities: A Survey of Recent Arguments and Evidence', *OECD Economic Studies*, Vol. 14, pp. 87-125.

Haskel, J. (1991): 'Imperfect Competition, Work Practices and Productivity Growth', *Oxford Bulletin of Economics and Statistics*, Vol. 53, pp. 265-79.

Hayward, K. (1983): *Government and British Civil Aerospace*, Manchester: Manchester University Press.

Hendry, J. (1989): *Innovating for Failure: Government Policy and the Early British Computer Industry*, London: MIT Press.

Heseltine, M. (1987): *Where There's a Will*, London: Hutchinson.

Hill, T. P. (1979): *Profits and Rates of Return*, Paris: OECD.

Hindley, B. (1983): 'What is the Case for State Investment Companies?', in B. Hindley (ed.), *State Investment Companies in Western Europe*, London: Macmillan.

Hindley, B. and Richardson, R. (1983): 'United Kingdom: An Experiment in Picking Winners—the Industrial Reorganisation Corporation', in B. Hindley (ed.), *State Investment Companies in Western Europe*, London: Macmillan.

Hitchens, D., Wagner, K. and Birnie, J. (1990): *Closing the Productivity Gap*, Aldershot: Avebury.

Horn, E-J. (1987): 'Germany: A Market-Led Process', in F. Duchene and G. Shepherd (eds.), *Managing Industrial Change in Western Europe*, London: Frances Pinter.

House of Lords (1985): *Report from the Select Committee on Overseas Trade*, London: HMSO.

House of Lords (1991): *Report from the Select Committee on Science and Technology*, London: HMSO.

Irwin, D. A. (1991): 'Terms of Trade and Economic Growth in Nineteenth Century Britain', *Bulletin of Economic Research*, Vol. 43, pp. 93-101.

Jaffe, A. (1986): 'Technological Opportunity and Spillovers of

R&D: Evidence from Firms' Patents, Profits and Market Value', *American Economic Review*, Vol. 76, pp. 984-1,001.

Jenkins, S. P. (1991): 'Income Inequality and Living Standards: Changes in the 1970s and 1980s', *Fiscal Studies*, Vol. 12, pp. 1-25.

Johnson, P. and Webb, S. (1992): 'Recent Trends in UK Income Inequality: Causes and Policy Responses', London: Institute for Fiscal Studies (mimeo).

Kaldor, N. (1966): *Causes of the Slow Rate of Growth of the United Kingdom*, Cambridge: Cambridge University Press.

Krugman, P. (1987): 'The Narrow Moving Band, the Dutch Disease, and the Competitive Consequences of Mrs Thatcher', *Journal of Development Economics*, Vol. 27, pp. 41-55.

Krugman, P. and Obstfeld, M. (1991): *International Economics*, 2nd edition, London: McGraw Hill.

Labour Party (1992): *Made in Britain*, London.

Layard, R., Nickell, S. and Jackman, R. (1991): *Unemployment*, Oxford: Oxford University Press.

Levitt, M. S. and Joyce, M. A. S. (1987): *The Growth and Efficiency of Public Spending*, Cambridge: Cambridge University Press.

Lucas, R. E. (1988): 'On the Mechanics of Economic Development', *Journal of Monetary Economics*, Vol. 22, pp. 3-42.

Machin, S. and Wadhwani, S. (1989): 'The Effects of Unions on Organizational Change, Investment and Employment: Evidence from WIRS', Centre for Labour Economics, London School of Economics Discussion Paper No. 355.

Maddison, A. (1989): *The World Economy in the Twentieth Century*, Paris: OECD.

Maddison, A. (1991): *Dynamic Forces in Capitalist Development*, Oxford: Oxford University Press.

Maizels, A. (1963): *Industrial Growth and World Trade*, Cambridge: Cambridge University Press.

Marsden, D. and Ryan, P. (1991): 'Initial Training, Labour Market Structure and Public Policy: Intermediate Skills in British and German Industry', in P. Ryan (ed.), *International*

Comparisons of Vocational Training for Intermediate Skills, Lewes: Falmer Press.

Matthews, R. C. O., Feinstein, C. H. and Odling-Smee, J. C. (1982): *British Economic Growth 1856-1973*, Oxford: Clarendon Press.

Mayer, C. (1992): 'The Financing of Innovation', in A. Bowen and M. Ricketts (eds.), *Stimulating Innovation in Industry*, London: Kogan Page.

Mayes, D. G. (1987): 'Does Manufacturing Matter?', *National Institute Economic Review*, No. 122, pp. 47-58.

Meeks, G. (1977): *Disappointing Marriage: A Study of the Gains from Merger*, Cambridge: Cambridge University Press.

Millward, R. (1990): 'Productivity in the UK Services Sector: Historical Trends 1856-1985 and Comparisons with the USA 1950-85', *Oxford Bulletin of Economics and Statistics*, Vol. 52, pp. 423-36.

Minami, R. (1986): *The Economic Development of Japan*, London: Macmillan.

Monopolies and Mergers Commission (1981): *Central Electricity Generating Board*, London: HMSO.

Monopolies and Mergers Commission (1983): *National Coal Board*, London: HMSO.

Montagnon, P. (1990): 'The Trade Policy Connection', in P. Montagnon (ed.), *European Competition Policy*, London: Frances Pinter Press.

Morris, D. J. and Stout, D. (1985): 'Industrial Policy', in D. J. Morris (ed.), *The Economic System in the UK*, Oxford: Oxford University Press.

Mowery, D. C. and Rosenberg, N. (1989): *Technology and the Pursuit of Economic Growth*, Cambridge: Cambridge University Press.

Muellbauer, J. and Murphy, A. (1990): 'Is the UK Balance of Payments Sustainable?', *Economic Policy*, Vol. 11, pp. 348-83.

Nelson, R. R. and Wright, G. (1992): 'The Rise and Fall of American Technological Leadership: The Postwar Era in

Historical Perspective', *Journal of Economic Literature*, Vol. 29, forthcoming.

Nordhaus, W. D. (1972): 'The Recent Productivity Slowdown', *Brookings Papers on Economic Activity*, Vol. 3, pp. 493-546.

Nordhaus, W. D. and Tobin, J. (1972): *Is Economic Growth Obsolete?*, New York: Columbia University Press.

OECD (1970): *National Accounts 1950-68*, Paris.

OECD (1984): *Industrial Structure Statistics*, 1982, Paris.

OECD (1989): *Economies in Transition*, Paris.

OECD (1991a): *Historical Statistics, 1960-1990*, Paris.

OECD (1991b): *Basic Science and Technology Statistics*, Paris.

OECD (1991c): *Employment Outlook*, Paris.

OECD (1992a): *Structural Change and Industrial Performance*, Paris.

OECD (1992b): *Industrial Structure Statistics, 1989/90*, Paris.

O'Higgins, M. and Jenkins, S. P. (1990): 'Poverty in the EC: 1975, 1980, 1985', in Eurostat, *Analyzing Poverty in the EC*, Luxembourg.

O'Mahony, M. (1992a): 'Productivity and Human Capital Formation in UK and German Manufacturing', National Institute of Economic and Social Research Discussion Paper No. 28.

O'Mahony, M. (1992b): 'Productivity Levels in British and German Manufacturing Industry', *National Institute Economic Review*, No. 139, pp. 46-63.

Olson, M. (1982): *The Rise and Decline of Nations*, New Haven: Yale University Press.

Oulton, N. (1992): 'Investment, Increasing Returns and the Pattern of Productivity Growth in UK Manufacturing, 1954-1986', National Institute of Economic and Social Research Discussion Paper No. 5.

Panic, M. (1976): *UK and West German Manufacturing Industry, 1954-1972: A Comparison of Performance and Structure*, London: NEDC.

Patel, P. and Pavitt, K. (1988): 'The International Distribution and Determinants of Technological Activities', *Oxford Review of Economic Policy*, Vol. 4(4), pp. 35-55.

Pavitt, K. and Soete, L. (1982): 'International Differences in Economic Growth and the International Location of Innovation', in H. Giersch (ed.), *Emerging Technologies*, Tubin: Mohr.

Peirce, W. (1991): 'Innovation and Diffusion in the "Single Europe"', *Technological Forecasting and Social Change*, Vol. 39, pp. 35-44.

Pilat, D. and Van Ark, B. (1991): 'Productivity Leadership in Manufacturing: Germany, Japan and the United States, 1973-1989', University of Groningen Faculty of Economics Research Memorandum No. 456.

Pomfret, R. (1991): 'The New Trade Theories, Rent-Snatching and Jet Aircraft', *The World Economy*, Vol. 14, pp. 269-77.

Prais, S. J. (1981): *Productivity and Industrial Structure*, Cambridge: Cambridge University Press.

Pratten, C. F. (1976): *Labour Productivity Differentials within International Companies*, Cambridge: Cambridge University Press.

Pratten, C. F. and Atkinson, A. G. (1976): 'The Use of Manpower in British Manufacturing Industry', *Department of Employment Gazette*, Vol. 84, pp. 571-76.

Pryke, R. (1981): *The Nationalised Industries*, Oxford: Martin Robertson.

Purcell, J. (1991): 'The Rediscovery of the Management Prerogative: The Management of Labour Relations in the 1980s', *Oxford Review of Economic Policy*, Vol. 7(1), pp. 33-43.

Rauch, J. E. (1991): 'Productivity Gains from Geographic Concentration of Human Capital: Evidence from the Cities', NBER Working Paper No. 3905.

Richardson, J. D. (1989): 'Empirical Research on Trade Liberalisation with Imperfect Competition', *OECD Economic Studies*, Vol. 12, pp. 7-50.

Rodrik, D. (1990): 'Soft Budgets, Hard Minds: Stray Thoughts on the Integration Process in Greece, Portugal and Spain', in

C. Bliss and J. B. Macedo (eds.), *Unity with Diversity in the European Economy: The Community's Southern Frontier*, Cambridge: Cambridge University Press.

Romer, P. M. (1986): 'Increasing Returns and Long-Run Growth', *Journal of Political Economy*, Vol. 94, pp. 1,002-1,037.

Romer, P. M. (1990): 'Human Capital and Growth: Theory and Evidence', *Carnegie-Rochester Conference Series on Public Policy*, Vol. 32, pp. 251-86.

Rowthorn, R. E. and Wells, J. R. (1987): *De-Industrialization and Foreign Trade*, Cambridge: Cambridge University Press.

Sargent, J. R. and Scott, M. (1986): 'Investment and the Tax System in the UK', *Midland Bank Review*, pp. 5-13.

Shackleton, J. R. (1992): *Training Too Much?*, Hobart Paper No. 118, London: Institute of Economic Affairs.

Shepherd, J. (1987): 'Industrial Support Policies', *National Institute Economic Review*, No. 122, pp. 59-71.

Silberston, A. (1981): 'Industrial Policies in Britain, 1960-1980', in C. F. Carter (ed.), *Industrial Policy and Innovation*, London: Heinemann.

Singh, A. (1975): 'Takeovers, Natural Selection and the Theory of the Firm: Evidence from Postwar UK Experience', *Economic Journal*, Vol. 85, pp. 497-515.

Smith, A. D., Hitchens, D. M. and Davies, S. W. (1982): *International Industrial Productivity*, Cambridge: Cambridge University Press.

Smith, R. P. (1990): 'Defence Procurement and Industrial Structure in the UK', *International Journal of Industrial Organization*, Vol. 8, pp. 185-205.

Soskice, D. (1989): 'Wage Determination: The Changing Role of Institutions in Advanced Industrialized Countries', *Oxford Review of Economic Policy*, Vol. 6(4), pp. 36-61.

Steedman, H. (1990): 'Improvement in Workforce Qualifications: Britain and France, 1979-88', *National Institute Economic Review*, No. 133, pp. 50-61.

Stoneman, P. (1991): 'The Promotion of Technical Progress in

[91]

UK Industry: A Consideration of Alternative Policy Instruments', Warwick Business School Research Papers No. 11.

Thirlwall, A. P. (1979): 'The Balance of Payments Constraint as an Explanation of International Growth Rate Differences', *Banca del Lavoro Quarterly Review*, Vol. 128, pp. 44-53.

Thirlwall, A. P. and Gibson, H. (1992): *Balance of Payments Theory and the UK Experience*, London: Macmillan.

Tolliday, S. and Zeitlin, J. (1991): 'National Models and International Variations in Labour Management and Employer Organization', in S. Tolliday and J. Zeitlin (eds.), *The Power to Manage?*, London: Routledge.

Turner, P., Coutts, A. and Bowden, S. (1992): 'The Effect of the Thatcher Government on Company Liquidations: An Econometric Study', *Applied Economics*, Vol. 24, pp. 935-43.

Ulman, L. (1968): 'Collective Bargaining and Industrial Efficiency', in R. Caves (ed.), *Britain's Economic Prospects*, Washington: Brookings Institution.

United Nations (1984): *International Trade Statistics Yearbook, 1982*, New York: UNO.

United Nations (1990): *International Trade Statistics Yearbook, 1988*, New York: UNO.

United States (1992): *Economic Report of the President*, Washington: Government Printing Office.

Van de Klundert, T. and Smulders, S. (1992): 'Reconstructing Growth Theory: A Survey', *De Economist*, Vol. 140, pp. 177-203.

Vickers, J. and Yarrow, G. (1988): *Privatization: An Economic Analysis*, London: MIT Press.

Wagner, K. (1991): 'Training Efforts and Industrial Efficiency in West Germany', in J. Stevens and R. McKay (eds.), *Training and Competitiveness*, London: Kogan Page.

Young, G. (1992): 'Industrial Investment and Economic Policy', in A. Britton (ed.), *Industrial Investment as a Policy Objective*, London: NIESR.